THE HISTORY OF THE THIRTEEN
COLONIES OF NORTH AMERICA

GEORGE WASHINGTON

FROM THE PAINTING ATTRIBUTED TO GILBERT STUART IN THE NATIONAL PORTRAIT GALLERY

THE HISTORY
OF THE THIRTEEN COLONIES
OF NORTH AMERICA

1497-1763

BY

REGINALD W. JEFFERY, M.A.

BRASENOSE COLLEGE, OXFORD

WITH EIGHT ILLUSTRATIONS AND A MAP

METHUEN & CO.
36 ESSEX STREET W.C.
LONDON

First Published in 1908

PREFACE

IT has been my object in this small book to put into a handy form a short narrative of the History of the Thirteen Colonies. In the limited space at my command I have endeavoured to give as often as possible the actual words of contemporaries, hoping that the reader may thereby be tempted to search further for himself amongst the mass of documentary evidence which still needs so much careful study. I cannot send this book into the world without acknowledging my indebtedness to both the Beit Professor of Colonial History, Mr H. E. Egerton, and the Beit Lecturer on Colonial History, Mr W. L. Grant, whose kind suggestions have proved most valuable. At the same time I must thank Mr E. L. S. Horsburgh, for by his action the writing of this little work was made possible.

R. W. J.

OXFORD, 1908

CONTENTS

CHAPTER I

INTRODUCTION : EARLY ENGLISH VOYAGES TO NORTH AMERICA

PAGE

Spanish, French, and Dutch colonisation—English colonisation—The Cabotian discoveries—The Cabots' second voyage—The Bull of Alexander VI.—The voyages of John Rut and Master Hore—Newfoundland Fishery—Cabot, Willoughby, and Chancellor—The attraction of the West—The North-West Passage—Martin Frobisher—Sir Humphrey Gilbert—Sir John Hawkins and Sir Francis Drake—Sir Walter Raleigh—The Elizabethan Period . 1

CHAPTER VI

THE FIGHT WITH THE DUTCH FOR THEIR SETTLEMENT OF NEW NETHERLANDS

CHAPTER VII

THE QUAKER SETTLEMENTS AND GEORGIA

CHAPTER VIII

THE SOCIAL AND ECONOMIC HISTORY OF NEW ENGLAND

CONTENTS

CHAPTER XII

THE CLIMAX : THE STRUGGLE BETWEEN ENGLISH AND FRENCH COLONISTS

LIST OF ILLUSTRATIONS

THE HISTORY OF
THE THIRTEEN COLONIES

CHAPTER I

INTRODUCTION: EARLY ENGLISH VOYAGES
TO NORTH AMERICA

IT would be out of place in this small book to give
in detail a history of all the discoveries which
were made along the shores of North and South
America at the end of the fifteenth and beginning of
the sixteenth centuries. As the main object is to
depict briefly the political history of the Thirteen
English Colonies on the North American seaboard,
it will be unnecessary to say more than a few words
about the discoverers whose enterprise and bravery
made colonisation possible. With the Spanish, French,
and Dutch voyagers it is not proposed to deal; their
stories are well known, and affected but little the
establishment of our early settlements in the West.
Like the British nation, these three peoples also strove
to create lasting empires in America; but unlike their
rival, they failed. The Spaniards made the fatal error
of attempting to settle during the period of exploration. They based their colonies upon slavery, and a
mistaken commercial policy; and the sparseness of
their colonists made them incapable of contending
against the pressure of surrounding savagery. The
result was that they, who were without the traditions

A   1

of public morality and who were to a certain extent lacking in administrative powers, became intermixed with the inferior races with whom they came in contact. The French were no more successful in their endeavours to establish a New France beyond the sea ; they failed, partly because of the French temperament, and partly through obvious errors. The French character was buoyant and cheerful—both excellent natural gifts for colonists—but they were unable to combine the spirit of adventure with that patient commercial industry which so wonderfully distinguished the Puritan emigrants. The Dutch might have proved serious rivals to the British in the West had they been able to rise from the position of mere traders, and had they had a sufficiently large population on which to draw. Their commercial system deteriorated, becoming uneconomic and non-progressive ; while their arduous and gallant struggle against Philip II. and Alva had necessarily handicapped them in the race for colonial aggrandisement.

The English, in strong contrast to these competitors, never drew a distinct or sharp line between the soldier and the trader. The story of Great Britain's expansion contains the names of hundreds of gallant heroes, but they were at the same time sober and industrious men. The plodding and commercial characteristics possessed by the British colonial saved him from perpetrating those foolish errors of the Spaniard which arose from a desire to gain rapid wealth and a tawdry glory. One fact stands out pre-eminent amongst the reasons of British success— the English kept their period of exploration almost entirely separate from their epoch of settlement. The glorious dreams of Eldorado, the visions of the golden

city of Manoa had been dispersed like a morning mist
when the period of colonisation dawned bright and
clear at the beginning of the seventeenth century.

The period which coincides with the reign of
Henry VII. forms one of the greatest epochs of
history ; it was indeed the veritable Renaissance, the
birth of the New World. It was at this moment that
the history of America, the modern history of England,
and the present history of Europe practically began.
These startling facts were due to the simultaneous
discoveries in the East and the West. The voyages
of Bartholomew Diaz, of Christopher Columbus, and
of Vasco de Gama might well have astonished the
world, but seem to have had very little effect upon the
English as a nation. England was not yet ready to
take up the position of Mistress of the Seas ; the
time was not yet ripe for colonial advancement. The
country, from both political and social points of view,
was still suffering from the confusion and anarchy
which had resulted from the rule of the Lancastrians,
and from the chaos left by the Wars of the Roses.
Two men, however, seem to have understood something of the possibilities that lay open to them in the
West. John and his son Sebastian Cabot, of Genoese
stock, but sometime resident in Venice, sailed, under
the patronage of Henry VII., from Bristol, in 1497, to
discover the island of Cathay. John Cabot is
described as one who had " made himself very expert
and cunning in knowledge of the circuit of the world
and Ilands of the same, as by a Sea card and other
demonstrations." [1] The royal charter, granted to these
men in March 1496, contained a most important
clause, " to saile to all parts, countreys, and seas of the

[1] *Hakluyt's Voyages* (ed. 1904), vii. p. 154.

East, of the West, and of the North, under our banners
and ensignes, . . . to set up our banners and ensignes
in every village, towne, castle, isle, or maine land of
them newly found . . . as our vassals, and lieutenants,
getting unto us the rule, title, and jurisdiction of the
same."[1]   Bacon, in his *History of Henry VII.*, refers
to Cabot's now celebrated voyage.   "There was one
Sebastian Gabato, a Venetian living in Bristow, a man
seen and expert in cosmography and navigation.
This man seeing the success and emulating perhaps
the enterprise of Christopherus Columbus in that
fortunate discovery towards the south-west, which had
been by him made some six years before, conceited
with himself that lands might likewise be discovered
towards the north-west.   And surely it may be that
he had more firm and pregnant conjectures of it than
Columbus had of his at the first.   For the two great
islands of the Old and New World, being in the shape
and making of them broad towards the north and
pointed towards the south, it is likely that the discovery just began where the lands did meet.   And
there had been before that time a discovery of some
lands which they took to be islands, and were indeed
of America towards the north-west."[2]   Bacon is here
calling attention to what has since become the great
controversial question of whether or not the Norsemen
discovered the American continent in the eleventh
century.   It is very improbable that the Cabots knew
anything of this tradition ; and this voyage was solely
the outcome of the discoveries of Columbus.   Their
object is definitely stated to have been a "great
desire to traffique for the spices as the Portingals

---

[1] *Hakluyt's Voyages*, vii. p. 143.
[2] *Bacon's Works* (ed. 1870), vi. 196.

did." [1] It is a remarkable fact that very little is known of this voyage, and there are practically no English records available in which to find the history of so great an event. A Bristol book contains this terse mention of the exploring expedition : " In the year 1497, the 24th of June, on St John's day, was Newfoundland found by Bristol men in a ship called the *Mathew*." [2] Carrying out the commands of the charter, John Cabot and his son planted the English standard upon American soil, but they did little besides : no explorations were made into the interior ; they were completely satisfied with the all-important fact of discovery. As a proof of their success, Sebastian Cabot brought back three Indians " in their demeanour like to bruite beastes," but who seem to have settled down and taken up English customs, for Robert Fabian says, " of the which upon two yeeres after, I saw two apparelled after the maner of Englishmen in Westminster pallace, which that time I could not discerne from Englishmen." [3]

The restless ambition of the Cabots incited them to a further voyage in February 1498, the charter on this occasion being granted only to the father. They again started from Bristol, and sailed along the North American coasts from the ice-bound shores of New-foundland [4] to the sunny Carolinas or Florida. The younger Cabot afterwards wrote that he sailed " unto the Latitude of 67 degrees and a halfe under the North Pole . . . finding still the open Sea without any maner of impediment, he thought verily by that

[1] *Hakluyt's Voyages* (ed. 1904), vii. p. 153.

[2] Barrett, *History and Antiquities of Bristol* (1789), p. 172.

[3] *Hakluyt's Voyages* (ed. 1904), vii. p. 155.

[4] It is thought by some that Cabot sailed to Greenland. Cf. Biggar *Voyages of the Cabots and of the Corte Reals* (Paris, 1903).

way to have passed on still the way to Cathaia which
is in the East."[1] This voyage is recorded by Sir
Humphrey Gilbert, and was frequently quoted as a
reason for England's claim to North America. "The
countreys lying north of Florida, God hath reserved
the same to be reduced unto Christian civility by the
English nation. For not long after that Christopher
Columbus had discovered the Islands and continent of
the West Indies for Spaine, John and Sebastian
Cabot made discovery also of the rest from Florida
northwards to the behoofe of England."[2] The
Cabots disappear from English history for a time and
there are no records of the reception of this voyage.
It was undoubtedly of twofold importance ; it started
that "will o' the wisp" of the North-West Passage,
that led so many men to risk and lose their lives ;
and it may also be regarded as the foundation-stone of
the English power in the West.

The next few years of the history of the exploration of America is filled with the records of Spaniards,
Italians, and Frenchmen. The voyage of the Bristol
merchants by which North America had just been
discovered had no effect, and awakened no enthusiasm
in the hearts of the English during the early portion
of the sixteenth century. Henry VII. and his more
adventurous son were both such severe and orthodox
Catholics that they hesitated to trespass upon the
limitations laid down by the bull of Alexander VI.,
by which everything on the western side of an
imaginary line between the forty-first and forty-fourth
meridians west of Greenwich belonged to Spain ;
while the Brazil coast, the East Indies, and Africa
south of the Canary Islands fell to Portugal. Between

[1] *Hakluyt's Voyages*, vii. p. 150.   [2] *Ibid.*, viii. p. 37.

1500 and 1550 only two true voyages of discovery have been chronicled. The first was in 1527, when a canon of St Paul's, erroneously named Albert de Prado, sailed with two ships in search of the Indies. It is probable that this was the voyage of John Rut of the Royal Navy, with whom, there is reason to suppose, a Spaniard, called Albert de Prado, sailed. They failed to make any real discoveries, but brought back a cargo of fish from the inhospitable shores of Newfoundland and Labrador. The second voyage was that of Master Hore, in 1536, who, it is supposed, set out in the spirit of a Crusader, but who was more probably a briefless barrister accompanied by " many gentlemen of the Innes of Court and of the Chancery." [1] They were shipwrecked on the Newfoundland coast, where, as none of them knew how to fish, and although Hore told them they would go to unquenchable fire, they began to eat one another. " On the fieldes and deserts here and there, the fellowe killed his mate, while he stooped to take up a roote for his reliefe, and cutting out pieces of his bodie whom he had murthered, broyled the same on the coles and greedily devoured them." [2] Luckily for the remainder, a French ship was blown into the harbour, and they seized her with all the food she had on board, sailing home in safety, leaving the French sailors to a horrible fate, which they seemed to have escaped ; for " certaine moneths after, those Frenchmen came into England and made complaint to King Henry the 8 : the king . . . was so mooved with pitie, that he punished not his subjects, but of his owne purse made full and royale recompense unto the French." [3]

[1] *Hakluyt's Voyages*, viii. p. 3.   [2] *Ibid.*, viii. p. 5.
[3] *Ibid.*, viii. p. 7.

The two voyages here set forth are the only ones that are actually recorded, but there is reason for supposing that English ships were quite familiar with the coast of what was afterwards called Maine. Between 1501 and 1510 there are many scattered intimations of English voyages; and one patent in particular, in the first year of the sixteenth century, shows that men of some importance were granted leave to sail and discover in the West. In 1503 a man brought hawks from Newfoundland to Henry VII.; and in the next year a priest is paid £2 to go to the same island. In or about the eighth year of Henry VIII., Sebastian Cabot was again in the employ of the English and in command of an expedition to Brazil, which only failed owing to "the cowardise and want of stomack" of his partner, Sir Thomas Pert.[1] It is evident from the first Act of Parliament relating to America, passed in 1541, that the Newfoundland fishery was carried on by Devonshire fishermen almost continuously from the discovery of the island; and the Act of 1548, prohibiting the exaction of dues, shows "that the trade out of England to Newfoundland was common."[2] Anthony Parkhurst corroborates this fact in a letter to Richard Hakluyt in 1578, in which he says, "The Englishmen, who commonly are lords of the harbors where they fish, and do use all strangers helpe in fishing if need require, according to an old custome of the countrey."[3] It may, therefore, be inferred that the growth of the Newfoundland fisheries, together with the increasing knowledge of the country and its products, helped to suggest to

[1] *Hakluyt's Voyages*, x. p. 2. [2] *Ibid.*, viii. p. 9.
[3] *Ibid.*, viii. p. 10.

the Englishmen of the period the possibilities of future colonisation.

The great voyager Sebastian Cabot returned to England in 1548 from his sojourn in Spain. Under the patronage of Charles V. he had made several voyages, including one of particular importance to the Rio de la Plata. On his arrival in England he was rewarded by Edward VI. with a pension of £166, 13s. 4d., as a slight evidence of that king's appreciation of his manifold services. Old man though he was, his mind still ran on the discovery of a North-West, or North-East Passage to the Indies, and he became the governor of a company of merchant adventurers for the discovery of regions beyond the sea. He did not participate in any of these discoveries, " because there are nowe many yong and lustie Pilots and Mariners of good experience, by whose forward-nesse I doe rejoyce in the fruit of my labours and rest with the charge of this office."[1] Amongst the young and lusty pilots were Sir Hugh Willoughby and Richard Chancellor, who turned their attentions to a North-East passage. The former died on his vessel in the midst of the ice floes in 1553, while the latter succeeded in reaching Archangel, and so brought about, through a successor, Anthony Jenkinson, the foundation of the Muscovy Company.

It was, however, the discovery of America, and in particular of the North-West Passage, that offered great inducements to Englishmen. The American continent had an ever fascinating attraction, for the reports of its vast wealth drew adventurous spirits as with a magnet. The gold of Mexico and Peru dazzled their eyes and made them hope to find

[1] *Hakluyt's Voyages*, vii. p. 149.

some similar hoard on every barren strip of shore
from Patagonia to Newfoundland.   " It was thought
that in those unknown lands, peopled by ' anthro-
pophagi and men whose heads did grow beneath their
shoulders,' lay all the treasures of the earth.   That
was an irresistible temptation to the great merchants
of England, citizens of no mean city, pursuing no
ignoble nor sordid trade." [1]   Thus early in the reign
of Elizabeth there was an attempt at American
plantation ; it certainly was only an attempt, for it
in no way furthered the schemes of colonisation.
Thomas Stukeley, a member of a good Devonshire
family, planned, with the sanction of the queen, in
1563, to colonise Florida.   He made the fatal mistake
of so many others, of converting a colonising expedition into one of mere buccaneering.   Spanish and
French vessels were his real objects, not the foundation of an English settlement in the New World.
The scheme naturally failed ; and Stukeley removed
his activities to Barbary, where he met a glorious
death amongst the chivalry of Portugal upon the
classic field of Alcazar.

The search for the North-West Passage was even
more tempting than the projection of imaginary
colonies in the South ; it opened before the eyes of
speculative voyagers a promise of all the wealth of
the East.   A large proportion of Hakluyt's great prose
epic—that marvellous work of adventure—is filled
with the search for Cathay.   That mystic land became
the purpose and the goal of hundreds of seamen who,
during the centuries, struggled and toiled through
overwhelming perils, ever to be baffled by the solid
and impenetrable ice.   Those wild north seas seem

[1] Fletcher, *Cornhill Magazine*, Dec. 1902.

to have caused little terror to the Tudor sea-dogs ; Master Thorne, for example, deserves to live in the memory of Englishmen for all time simply for one remark with which he is credited. When the objection of the ice was proposed to him, he waived it on one side with words which might well be taken as the motto of the British Empire : " There is no land unhabitable and no sea innavigable." [1] Sir Humphrey Gilbert, in particular, tried to encourage men to push forward in their adventurous discoveries, and there is no doubt that his famous work, *A Discourse to prove a passage by the North West to Cathaya and the East Indies*, did a great deal to stimulate men in their hopeless task.

It was largely due to this *Discourse* that Martin Frobisher sailed to find the tantalising passage, in June 1576, under the patronage of the all-powerful Earl of Warwick. He sighted Greenland, and then reached that inlet on the American coast which he called Frobisher Bay. He brought back with him samples of a black stone which were supposed to contain gold, and thus added the temptation of easily acquired wealth to the sufficiently delusive and dangerous task of discovering the passage. The possibility of mineral wealth in the Arctic Regions brought about the formation of the Company of Cathay, under the government of Michael Lok ; and as its Captain-General, Frobisher undertook a second voyage in May 1577. His object was " the further discovering of the passage to Cathay, and other Countreys, thereunto adjacent, by West North-West navigations : which passage or way is supposed to bee on the North and North-West part of America . . .

[1] *Hakluyt's Voyages*, ii. p. 178.

where through our Merchants may have course and recourse with their merchandise." [1] Frobisher took possession of the barren territory, and on his return Queen Elizabeth "named it very properly Meta Incognita, as a marke and bound utterly hitherto unknown." [2] The gold-refiners of London were still deceived by the black stones ; and again Frobisher sailed, in May 1578, to work this imaginary mine. He took with him on this occasion "a strong fort or house of timber" for the shelter of "one hundreth persons, whereof 40 should be mariners for the use of ships, 30 Miners for gathering the gold Ore together for the next yere, and 30 souldiers for the better guard of the rest, within which last number are included the Gentlemen, Gold finers, Bakers, Carpenters & all necessary persons." [3] This might be regarded as an early attempt to found a colony, for Frobisher seems to have hoped to establish a thriving industry in this desolate and ice-bound land ; but as a matter of fact these "necessary persons" did nothing at all except to discover an island which existed only in their imaginations, and they returned to England in the autumn. Frobisher's efforts as a discoverer now ceased ; for his seamanship and courage were required in home waters for the protection of his native land.

Sir Humphrey Gilbert, half-brother of Raleigh, was the "first of our nation that carried people to erect an habitation and government in those northerly countreys of America." [4] He was a man bold in action and chivalrous in character ; he was one of those giants of the Elizabethan period, and if he had any faults they were only those of his age, while his virtues

[1] *Hakluyt's Voyages*, vii. p. 212.   [2] *Ibid.*, vii. p. 320.
[3] *Ibid.*, vii. p. 321.   [4] *Ibid.*, vii. p. 38.

were all his own.   As early as 1563 he was connected
with schemes for colonisation in the formation of a
company for the discovery of new trades.   He it is
who has the proud position of being the founder of
our premier colony, Newfoundland.   In 1578, letters
patent were granted to him by Queen Elizabeth for
establishing a colony in North America.   He made
his first voyage in that year, sailing from Dartmouth
in September.   The expedition was a complete failure,
and fearing lest his patent should expire, he undertook that voyage which has made him one of the
most famous men in history.   In 1583 he sailed to
Newfoundland, and took possession in the name of
the Virgin Queen, " and signified unto al men, that
from that time forward, they should take the same
land as a territorie appertaining to the Queene of
England." [1]   His great action was not allowed to be
forgotten ; the gallant knight himself never saw
England again, but passed to his grave beneath the
rough waters of the Atlantic.   Hakluyt, however,
printed the story of an eye-witness, Edward Hayes,
who gave a graphic account of the whole expedition.
Gilbert insisted on returning in the *Squirrel,* a small
crazy craft, rather than in the larger vessel, known as
the *Hinde.*   The weather became very foul ; and on
Monday afternoon, the 9th of September, Hayes says,
" the frigate was neere cast away oppressed by the
waves, yet at that time recovered : and giving foorth
signes of joy the Generall, sitting abaft with a
booke in his hand cried out unto us in the Hind (so oft
as we did approach within hearing) We are as neere
to heaven by sea as by land."   About twelve that
night, the frigate being ahead of the Hinde, her

[1] *Hakluyt's Voyages,* viii. p. 54.

lights suddenly went out; and after a minute's awful
silence, the men of the Hinde exclaimed, "the General
was cast away."[1] Thus the hero, strong in his belief
and fear of God, with chivalrous and stainless name,
found his last resting-place in the sea. He was a
forerunner of the very noblest type, an example to
the men of his own generation, and to those fearless
adventurers who have helped to create the British
Empire in all parts of the world.

The northern portions of America were for the most
part more easily accessible to the English, and the
dangers of Spanish and Portuguese attacks were more
remote. The West Indies, however, and even South
America, were not without their fascination, and
many Englishmen made voyages to those parts, not
so much for the purposes of discovery as for trade,
buccaneering, and booty. The earliest of these West
Indian trading voyages was that of Thomas Tison,
who, it is known, sailed to the West, some time
previous to the year 1526. He dwelt on one of the
West Indian Islands as a secret factor for some
English merchants; and "it is probable that some of
our marchants had a kinde of trade to the West
Indies even in those ancient times and before also:
neither doe I see," says Hakluyt, "any reason why
the Spaniards should debarre us from it at this
present."[2] As a trader, pirate, and slave-dealer, Sir
John Hawkins made three celebrated voyages in
1562, 1564, and 1568, between Guinea and the West
Indies. On one of these he was accompanied by
Francis Drake, who was destined for far greater
things than slave-dealing. After many adventures off
the Spanish main, Drake, in the spirit of a Crusader,

[1] *Hakluyt's Voyages*, viii. p. 74.   [2] *Ibid.*, x. pp. 6, 7.

SIR FRANCIS DRAKE

FROM AN ENGRAVING BY I. HOUBRAKEN

started on his momentous voyage round the world.
In a small vessel called the *Golden Hinde* or *Pelican*,
with a still smaller ship, the *Elizabeth*, the great
seaman sailed from Plymouth in February 1577.
Sailing down the South American coast, he at last
arrived at the Straits of Magellan, where one of his
company, Master Thomas Doughty, mutinied and was
executed.   After being deserted by the *Elizabeth*, the
voyage proceeded along the shores of Chili and Peru ;
and passing still farther north, it is probable that
Drake discovered "that portion of North America
now known as Oregon, and anticipated by centuries
the progress of English colonisation : the New
Albion, which he took over from the Indians, being
probably the British Columbia of to-day."[1]   Drake's
return was made without any very serious mishaps,
and he dropped anchor in Plymouth Sound in
November 1580.   It was a fine exploit, and roundly
applauded throughout the country.   No one, however,
realised at that time, nor indeed for generations to
come, that Drake had discovered and annexed what
was afterwards to become so large a portion of the
British dominions beyond the seas.

One man in particular could not fail to be moved
to enthusiasm by these voyages of discovery.   The
dream of a great country in the far West, peopled by
the Anglo-Saxon race, was ever before the eyes of Sir
Walter Raleigh.   The character of this great man of
action was not without many faults, for it was composed of much fine gold tempered with clay.   His
endeavours, however, to extend the limits of Britain's
rule excite the imagination and entrance the mind of
the reader.   The mantle of Gilbert fell upon the

[1] Egerton, *Origin and Growth of the English Colonies*, p. 65.

shoulders of Raleigh, who at once attempted to carry
on the work of colonisation which had been started by
his half-brother in Newfoundland ; and the road to
which was about to be pointed out by Richard
Hakluyt in his *Discourse of Western Planting.*
Raleigh must have appreciated the appeal made by
Sir George Peckham, friend of Gilbert, when he said,
" Behold heere, good countreymen, the manifold benefits,
commodities and pleasures heretofore unknowen, by
Gods especiall blessing not onely reveiled unto us, but
also as it were infused into our bosomes, who though
hitherto like dormice have slumbered in ignorance
thereof, being like the cats that are loth for their prey
to wet their feet : yet if now therefore at the last we
would awake, and with willing mindes (setting
frivolous imaginations aside) become industrious
instruments to ourselves, questionlesse we should not
only hereby set forth the glory of our heavenly father,
but also easily attaine to the end of all good purposes
that may be wished or desired." [1]   Up to this time, by
a curious chance, the coastline of the modern United
States, from the St Lawrence to the Savannah River,
had scarcely been visited and was, in fact, very little
known.   Here then was an opportunity for Raleigh ;
and a land, where, if effort was made, the greatest
success might be achieved.   The land had been
unspoilt and untouched by the Spaniards ; those few
hardy seamen who had entered harbour or creek had
found no signs of gold, and had sailed away again.
But it was a land of excellent climate, freed from the
ice and fogs of the more northern latitudes in which
the Elizabethan seamen had shown such pluck and
powers of endurance.   Captain Carlile, the son-in-law

[1] *Hakluyt's Voyages* (ed. 1904), viii. p. 123.

of Francis Walsingham, had already in 1583 issued his encouraging report concerning American trade. Raleigh could not fail to be struck by the sentence, " that whereas one adventureth in the great enterprise, an hundred for that one will of themselves bee willing and desirous to adventure in the next." [1] Gilbert's patent for the colonisation of North America had been transferred to Raleigh, who, with great caution, in 1584 dispatched two sea-captains, Amidas and Barlow, to spy out this land of promise. The narrative of these adventurers as given in *Hakluyt's Voyages* is extremely picturesque. They steered a more southerly course than that of any previous British explorer, and finally reached the island of Roanoke, now within the limits of North Carolina. They described it as a land flowing with milk and honey. " The second of July, we found shole water, wher we smelt so sweet and so strong a smel, as if we had been in the midst of some delicate garden abounding with all kinde of odoriferous flowers. . . . We found the people most gentle, loving, and faithfull, voide of all guile and treason, and such as live after the maner of the golden age." [2] Amidas and Barlow thus brought back to their patron Raleigh a story full of hope and wondrous possibilities. They had found a land worthy of colonisation and well suited to the English ; and this land of promise and of future greatness was christened by the Virgin Queen—Virginia.

The days of exploration and discovery by sea in the West had practically come to an end ; the great epoch of colonisation was about to begin. When Elizabeth came to the throne, English ships had

[1] *Hakluyt's Voyages* (ed. 1904), viii. p. 141.
[2] *Ibid.*, viii. pp. 298 and 305.

B

seldom sailed further than Iceland in the north and the Levant in the south-east, where a lucrative trade had sprung up as early as 1511. But by the end of the sixteenth century, owing to the encouragement of the Tudor sovereigns, the religious persecutions, and the " peculiar " policy of Elizabeth, the English flag had been proudly borne into all the seas of the world. The globe had been circumnavigated by Drake and Cavendish ; trade through Archangel had been established with Russia ; spices had been brought from the Indies by the East India Company ; " the commodious and gainful voyage to Brazil "[1] was regularly undertaken by the merchants of Southampton ; while a vast fishing trade had steadily grown up off the coasts of Newfoundland. Above all the " navigations, voyages, traffiques, and discoveries of the English nation " had laid the foundation for greater things. Raleigh's dreams were to be accomplished, though not by himself. Like so many others he was attracted by gold ; his thoughts lay too readily in the discovery of an El Dorado in South America, of which the Elizabethan poet wrote :—

> " Guiana whose rich feet are mines of gold."

The grain of mustard seed had, however, been planted ; the idea had been put forth to the world ; a new nation was to rise in the Western hemisphere ; and, although no definite results were to be seen by the eyes of the Elizabethans, yet their wild adventures, their acts of knight-errantry, their perils and their sufferings had paved the way for the industrious, sober, steady, and more prudent enterprises of Stuart Cavaliers and of Puritan Pilgrims.

[1] *Hakluyt's Voyages*, xi. p. 25.

CHAPTER II

VIRGINIA: THE FIRST GREAT COLONY OF THE BRITISH

THE English settlers in America may be less romantic and less interesting figures than their Elizabethan predecessors, but they were undoubtedly fitter instruments for the specific work. The Elizabethan seamen had played their part, and men now arose who were to fulfil a greater destiny. The Gilberts and the Drakes were of a race which had ceased to be, and Fuller justly remarks " how God set up a generation of military men both by sea and land which began and expired with the reign of Queen Elizabeth, like a suit of clothes made for her and worn out by her ; for providence so ordered the matter that they almost all attended their mistress before or after, within some short distance, unto her grave." [1] Although the adventurous spirit of the Golden Age had passed away, men were still left who could echo the words of Sir Humphrey Gilbert and say, " and therefore to give me leave without offence always to live and die in this mind, that he is not worthy to live at all that for fear or danger of death shunneth his country's service and his own honour, seeing death is inevitable and the

---

[1] Quoted by Professor Raleigh in Introduction to *Hakluyt's Voyages* (ed. 1904), xii. p. 24.

fame of virtue immortal." [1] The one great figure who appears to connect the old period with the new was Sir Walter Raleigh. As has already been mentioned, he had sent out an expedition in 1584 to see what possibility there was of establishing a colony in America. The glowing accounts brought back by his two captains made Raleigh decide upon an undertaking which, though it proved a failure, must ever be regarded as memorable in the world's history.

In 1585 Raleigh sent seven ships and one hundred and eight settlers to the land which had been granted to him by patent. The territory had already been named Virginia, in honour of the Queen, and it was here that he hoped to establish a little colony composed of sturdy Englishmen. In June the settlers, having landed in Roanoke, were left under the leadership of Ralph Lane ; the other generals, Grenville, Cavendish, and Amidas, returning to the mother country. From the outset it was certain that Raleigh's colony must fail. The man chosen as leader had no special aptitude for the post, being possessed with the mania for discovery rather than the desire to teach the settlers to form a self-supporting community. But even worse than this, Lane made the fatal error of estranging the natives by the severity and brutality of his punishments. Exactly a year after the settlers had landed, Sir Francis Drake put in to see how his friend Raleigh's Utopian schemes progressed. He found the colony in a miserable plight and, yielding to the earnest entreaties of the settlers, took them on board and sailed to England. Raleigh, however, had not forgotten his colony, and had dispatched Sir Richard Grenville with supplies ; but when he reached

[1] *Hakluyt's Voyages* (ed. 1904), vol. vii. p 190.

the settlement he found it deserted. Sir Walter
Raleigh's buoyant nature was not depressed by this
first failure, and in 1587 a fresh attempt to settle
Virginia was made. Under the command of White,
one hundred and thirty-three men and seventeen
women were sent out. White soon returned to
England for supplies, leaving his daughter Eleanor
Dare, who gave birth to the first white child born in
the New World. The unhappy emigrants received but
little assistance from the home authorities. Certainly
two expeditions were sent out to help them, but they
failed because their captains found it more lucrative
and exciting to go privateering. The stirring times
in Europe and the coming of the Armada were sufficient
to absorb the minds of such men as Raleigh and
Drake, and the colony in Virginia was left to its fate.
What that fate was can only be imagined, for, when
White at last reached Virginia in 1589, not a trace of
the colony was to be found, while another expedition
in 1602 proved equally unsuccessful in the search.
Hunger and the Indians had done their cruel work, and
the hand of destiny seemed turned against the foundation of an Anglo-Saxon colony in the mysterious
West.

There were, however, dominant motives for colonisation at the beginning of the seventeenth century, and
these, together with the intrepidity of certain of the
Elizabethan school, changed the aspect of the whole
question. The previous incentives for discovery and
adventure upon the high seas had been the tricks of
imagination, the more glorious scheme of spreading
Christianity and the race for gold. But now there
was a fear amongst the more intellectual thinkers
in England that the country was suffering from a

surplus population. This purely imaginary danger gave birth to the idea that America might provide new homes for this surplus, and, at the same time, bring new markets into existence which in the future would very materially help to develop the naval resources of the English.

One of the most able and energetic of the new patrons of colonisation was Shakespere's friend, the Earl of Southampton, who in March 1602 dispatched to the West, Bartholomew Gosnold with thirty-two companions. This little band of adventurers landed further north than Raleigh's ill-fated colonists, probably at a spot where in later years the Puritan settlers established themselves. The chief feature of Gosnold's venture was the discovery of a new route to the West by way of the Azores, and thus a week was saved in future voyages. In the following year the *Discovery* and *Speedwell* were sent out under Martin Pring, the patrons of the expedition having first obtained formal permission from Sir Walter Raleigh, whose patent rights were still regarded as valid. It is interesting to notice that with this concession on Raleigh's part his connection with Virginia ceased for ever.

One of Pring's patrons was Richard Hakluyt, to whom all Englishmen are indebted for his great prose epic and for the stimulus he gave to the early founders of the British Empire. Hakluyt was born in London about the year 1552. He was educated at Westminster School and Christ Church, Oxford, where he took his degree in 1574. His interest in geography and discovery had been aroused when quite a boy by seeing a map in the possession of a relative, and from that moment, he writes, " I constantly resolved, if ever I was preferred to the University,

where better time and more convenient place might
be ministred for those studies, I would, by God's
assistance, prosecute that knowledge and kinde of
literature, the doores whereof (after a sort) were so
happily opened before me." [1] Hakluyt's first book was
published in 1582, under the title, *Divers Voyages
touching the discoverie of America and the Ilands
adjacent unto the same, made first of all by Englishmen
and afterwards by the Frenchmen and Britons.* This
work consisted of a collection of documents to support
England's claim to the prior discovery of America.
In the autumn of 1584 he presented to Queen
Elizabeth his *Discourse of Western Planting*, the
writing of which was largely due to the inspiration of
Sir Walter Raleigh. The subject matter had been
supplied by the two voyagers to Virginia, Captains
Amidas and Barlow. The first edition of his great
work saw light in the year after the Armada; but
Hakluyt was not satisfied, and for nine more years
laboured on, until in 1598 he produced the second
edition in three volumes, and the world was in-
finitely the richer for the *Principal Navigations,
Voyages, Traffiques, and Discoveries of the English
Nation.*

The year that Hakluyt sent out Pring to make
discoveries is ever famous for the death of Queen
Elizabeth. The great queen, whatever her faults may
have been, had indeed bound her subjects to her by
affection and admiration, and created amongst them a
remarkable spirit of both patriotism and gallantry. It
was therefore a fitting and happy circumstance that
associated the last of the Tudors with the first of our
American colonies. Virginia, named from Elizabeth,

[1] *Hakluyt's Voyages* (ed. 1904), vol. i. p. xviii.

the child, so to speak, of a queen, came in time to be the mother of Presidents. It is not, however, until the accession of the pedantic James that a stern resolve to accomplish the establishment of a colony seems to have been taken. The irony of history is better illustrated in this fact than perhaps elsewhere. The mean mind and timid heart of James I. could never arouse or inspire enthusiasm as Elizabeth's actions had done. And yet the appreciation of the importance of a great Empire was reserved for the reign of the first Stuart rather than during the rule of the greatest of the Tudors.

The pressing question of surplus population which had reached a climax at the accession of James I., together with the prosperity and success of the newly formed East India Company may have had something to do with the momentous decision that was taken in 1606. In that year two companies were formed : the first was the London Company, which was given permission by the Crown to plant in North America between 45° and 38° north latitude ; the second division was the Plymouth Company, whose rights of plantation overlapped those of the London Company, their district being between 41° and 34° north latitude. With the history of this second company we shall deal later.

The London Company consisted of various members, such as Richard Hakluyt, the recorder of voyages ; Sir George Somers, " a lamb on shore, a lion at sea" ; [1] and Sir Thomas Gates. The Council was nominated by the King, and included many well-known men of the day ; in particular, Sir Ferdinando Gorges, who played an important part in colonial history for

[1] Quoted by Doyle, *The English in America*, Virginia (1882), p. 145.

many years,[1] and Sir Edwin Sandys, who, in the perilous time which came upon the Company, fought manfully for the right. The system of administration was of considerable complexity, as the control of affairs was both divided and qualified. In return for finding the capital for the proper working of the scheme, the Company was to receive certain trading privileges. The actual government was vested in two councils, both of which were nominated by James I., the one to be resident in England and supreme in all political and legislative affairs, the other to be established in the colony and liable for the proper administration of all local matters. The orders given to those in office, when the first settlement was made, were to a certain extent harsh, but in no way contrary to the spirit of the times. The Church of England was to be supported and the supremacy of the King to be acknowledged. All serious crimes were to be tried by jury and punished with death, but the penalty for minor offences was left to the discretion of the resident council. The Company took care that no trade was carried on by private individuals, and it was insisted that magazines should be erected for the produce of the colony and for supplying necessities to the colonists. It may be stated finally that the old ideas of enterprise and adventure were not lost sight of, and what had stirred Columbus and many another voyager was now definitely mentioned in the commands. The settlers were told " to show kindness to the savages and heathen people in those parts, and use all proper means to draw them to the true knowledge and service of God." [2]

[1] *American Historical Review*, vol. iv. No. 4, pp. 678-702.
[2] Quoted by Doyle, *op. cit.*, p. 147.

By the middle of December 1606, one hundred and forty-three colonists [1] were on board three ships ready to sail for their new home in the West. On the morning of New Year's Day, 1607, the little fleet sailed down the Thames. All praise be to them for showing so brave a spirit in launching out into an unknown world at the very dawn of England's expansion. And yet it must be acknowledged that they were the very worst type of settlers that could have been chosen for such an undertaking. They were idle, discontented, impatient, and incapable. Many of them were gentlemen, who had no idea of manual labour ; some were goldsmiths and jewellers, who were without knowledge of agriculture, building, or even protecting themselves from savages. But even worse than this was the fact that they had no leader with natural gifts for so important a position. At their head, to begin with, was Christopher Newport, famous as a raider off the Spanish main. In council with him were Gosnold, the intrepid voyager, and Captain John Ratcliffe, a discontented man, as proved by his later actions, although a contemporary describes him as "a very valiant, honest, and painful soldier." [2] From the very outset there were quarrels, and Captain John Smith, whom we shall meet again, was kept in confinement during the greater part of the voyage.

On the 16th April 1607, the storm-tossed adventurers sighted the southernmost extremity of Chesapeake Bay, and called it Cape Henry in honour of the Prince of Wales. On the 13th May they selected a place for settlement, and Jamestown, the

[1] Doyle says 143 colonists ; neither Percy nor Newport mention the exact number ; Bradley, in his life of *Captain John Smith*, says 105.

[2] *Cf.* footnote, Doyle, *op. cit.*, p. 149.

first permanent plantation, was established in Virginia on the James River. Almost immediately Edward Maria Wingfield was elected president, which proved to be one of the many mistakes made by the settlers. Nobody can question Wingfield's bravery, honesty, and desire to act justly, but it is very evident from the records that he was formal and pompous in manner, and filled with a too conscious sense of his own dignity. No sooner had the president been elected than the colony was weakened by a division of their party. Captain John Smith with a few followers preferred to accompany Newport on an exploring expedition, and reached a spot where now stands Richmond City. The Indians, under their leader Powhattan, appeared friendly to this party, but native friendship could only bear a slight strain, and trouble was only too likely to arise from the careless conduct of the settlers who had remained at Jamestown. The time was passed in a series of petty squabbles, and the infant colony struggled through a period of the gravest vicissitudes. Gosnold, one of the best of the party, died, and this was followed by the deposition of Wingfield, Captain Ratcliffe being made governor in his place. His period of office was marked by troubles with the Indians, and dire sickness which broke out amongst the settlers, owing to bad water, want of food, and the unhealthy situation of Jamestown.

At last the dominant character of Captain John Smith manifested itself, and he was chosen chief by common consent. This man's remarkable adventures read like fiction, but there is little doubt that there is a great deal of truth in all that he has left on record. Some of the most romantic episodes that he lays before the reader may perhaps be regarded as exaggerations or even untrustworthy, but it would be entirely erroneous to look upon him as a mere Baron Munchausen or a foolish braggart. He was brave beyond words, robust in person and self-reliant in mind. In all his actions he was public-spirited, and, at the same time, for his age and for his training, tolerant, kindly, and humane. He was one of the most romantic figures of the period, and as such appeals in his narrative to the sympathy of his readers and captures their affection. As a soldier in the wars in the Netherlands he had passed through many a danger. As a traveller in France, Italy, and the near East he had learnt to understand and command men. As a hardy crusader and captain in the Turkish wars he had fought manfully against the infidel in Hungary. He had suffered all the horrors of slavery, from which he had escaped through the forests of Transylvania. This man of many adventures may be regarded by posterity as the chief promoter of the colonisation of Virginia, and, if not her founder, at least her saviour.

The early settlers in Virginia would have suffered the fate of Raleigh's colony of 1587 had it not been for Captain John Smith's perseverance, steady courage, and determination. He struggled hard to teach the colonists the necessity of making themselves a self-sufficing community. Most of the men thought that gold was to be picked up anywhere, failing to see that if they did not strive manfully they must inevitably starve. Smith himself says, " our diet is a little meal and water, and not sufficient of that ";[1] and his words are proved by the fact that within the past six months fifty of the colonists died, and to use the words of the chronicler, " for the most part they died of famine."

[1] Smith's Letter to the Virginia Company.

Smith determined that this should not continue, and he took for his motto, " Nothing is to be expected except by labour." Excellent as was the motto, the material from which he had to build up a colony was of the very worst, and it is only natural that he should write home and ask for " thirty carpenters, blacksmiths, masons, and diggers up of trees' roots, rather than a thousand of such as we have." [1] His past experiences now stood him in good stead, and he proved himself a capable leader by succeeding in forcing the colony into a small, settled community. When he felt that the colony was for the time being fairly secure he went on exploring expeditions among the Indians. This was part of the purpose and duty of the colony, for men were eager to find a short passage to India, and no one imagined that America was of the gigantic size that later discovery proved it to be. Whilst on these expeditions the adventures of Smith were most extraordinary, and may possibly have been coloured by lapse of time and a brilliant imagination. Once he saved his life by the marvels of his compass and by the writing of notes to his friends in Jamestown ; and once indeed, according to his own record, he was saved by the lovely Pocahontas, who pleaded with her father Powhattan for his life. This latter story is, however, extremely unlikely, for the Indian princess could have been only a child at the time, and it is probable that Smith added the account when the fame of Pocahontas had spread to Europe.

Smith spent the whole of the spring of 1609 in Jamestown endeavouring to make the settlers industrious by prosecuting the manufacture of tar, pitch, and soap ashes. Up to this time, with absurd care

---

[1] Quoted by Bradley, *Captain John Smith* (1905), p. 144.

lessness, the Jamestown fortification had been left without a well, and Smith now remedied this obvious defect. With equal energy he turned to building, and during the months of February, March, and April, he erected twenty houses, besides a blockhouse, and re-roofed the church. Agriculture and the fishing industry were no longer neglected, and while some of the settlers under Smith's guidance brought forty acres under cultivation, others undertook to supply the colony with fish. Struggle as he did, Smith continually suffered reverses, and many disasters overtook the colonists, the most serious being the destruction of their corn by rats. Starvation stared them in the face, but Smith's firmness and activity overcame the horrors of famine, and instead of allowing the settlers to mass together, the men were quartered in different localities where they had to seek food for themselves. When this remarkable man at last left the colony, it can scarcely be said to have been in a prosperous state, but there were four hundred and ninety strong colonists who had been put on the right road towards progress, partly by Smith's example and partly by his doctrine " that he who would not work might not eat."

About the time that Smith was preparing to return to England there was in that country a reawakening of interest in what Drayton called, " Virginia, earth's only Paradise." The keener interest that was now being shown was largely due to a number of pamphlets that had been published, and also to the enthusiastic sermons of many of the clergy of the day. In a pamphlet named the *Nova Britannia* it was pointed out that Virginia was a valuable opening as a new market for English cloth, and, in addition, that trade between the two countries would stimulate the

THE PORTRAICTUER OF CAPTAYNE IOHN SMITH
ADMIRALL OF NEW ENGLAND.

Ætat 37
A° 1616

These are the Lines that shew thy Face; but those
That shew thy Grace and Glory, brighter bee:
Thy Faire-Discoueries and Fowle-Overthrowes
Of Salvages, much Civilliz'd by thee
Best shew thy Spirit; and to it Glory Wyn;
So, thou art Brasse without, but Golde within.

CAPTAIN JOHN SMITH
FROM HIS "GENERALL HISTORIE OF VIRGINIA"

merchant navy. " We shall not still betake ourselves
to small and little shipping as we daily do beginne,
but we shall rear againe such Marchants Shippes,
both tall and stout, as no forreine sayle that swimmes
shall make them vayle or stoop ; whereby to make
this little northern corner of the world to be in a
short time the richest storehouse and staple for
marchandise in all Europe." [1] With this idea of
making England "the richest storehouse," a new
charter was granted to the Company in May 1609.
The London Company was now put under a number
of influential men, including Robert Cecil, Earl of
Salisbury, and Sir Francis Bacon, while at the same
time the old directors remained upon the board. Under
the new charter the dual control of the two councils
disappeared, and the government was to be in the
hands of one council nominated in the first case by
the King, and afterwards, as vacancies occurred, they
were to be filled by men elected by the Company.
The powers of the Company were also extended, for
besides the right of levying duties, it was conceded
that defensive war might be waged if it were thought
expedient. By these means the Company practically
became an independent body.

The outcome of the change was immediately seen
in an expedition which set out under Sir George
Somers and Sir Thomas Gates. In July 1609 these
adventurers were wrecked upon the uninhabited
Bermudas, but in the following spring they succeeded
in reaching Virginia. The attractive picture of the
settlement as drawn in pamphlet and sermon in
England was scarcely true to life. As a matter of
fact no sooner had Smith left the colony than its

---

[1] Force, *Tracts* (1836-46), vol. i.

inhabitants dropped back into their slothful ways, which were at once taken advantage of by the cunning Redskins, who, peaceful while the great captain was present, had now become most hostile. Thus Sir Thomas Gates in this year records, " the state of the Colony . . . began to find a sensible declyning: which Powhattan (as a greedy Vulture) obseruing, and boyling with desire of reuenge, he inuited Captaine Ratclife and about thirty others to trade foɪ Corne, and vnder the colour of fairest friendship he brought them within the compasse of his ambush, whereby they were cruelly murthered and massacred." [1]

The fate of the colony once more hung in the balance ; starvation was once again at the door. Very fortunately for the settlers, Lord Delawarr arrived as Captain-General and Governor, with, what was most important, supplies. The Company, how- ever was becoming disheartened. The colony had now been in existence for three years and the returns to the shareholders were meagre indeed. Something had to be done and strong measures seemed appro- priate. In June 1611, Delawarr embarked for England, but Sir Thomas Dale had already been dispatched with the title of High Marshal of Virginia. He was armed with a military and civil code of the greatest severity, for he was confronted with the arduous task of governing a people made up of " the scourings of London." The military code was from the first practically a dead letter ; but the civil enactments were so extremely harsh and so peculiar to modern ideas that they deserve some attention. Daily worship according to the service of the Church

[1] Gates, *A True Declaration of the Estate of the Colonie in Virginia* (1610).

of England was enforced by a penalty of six months
in the galleys. To refrain from attending Sunday
service meant death. If any man " unworthily demean
himself unto any preacher or minister of God's word "
he was to be openly whipped three times, and after
each whipping he was to confess his crime. But
these laws were almost mild in comparison with the
vague and brutal enactment that " no man shall give
disgraceful words or commit any act to the disgrace
of any person in this colony, or any part thereof,
upon pain of being tied head and feet together
upon the ground every night for the space of one
month." [1]

These harsh laws continued, but did not affect the
tide of emigration from England. In August 1611,
Sir Thomas Gates returned as Governor with three
hundred fresh settlers.[2] From this moment a much
better class of colonists began to come out, bringing
with them their own servants, and forming the nucleus
of a sound colonial population. There were, of course,
other reasons for the improved state of affairs, not
the least important being the fact that Gates worked
hard for the benefit of the colony. An excellent
change was carried out when the settlers deserted
unhealthy Jamestown for the more salubrious Henrico.
Here a church, a hospital, and good houses of brick
were erected, and a palisade was raised as a protection
from the Indians. Industries, too, began to thrive, for
the records show that both silk and iron were manu-
factured, while vines were cultivated with success by

[1] Force, *Tracts* (1836-46), vol. iii.
[2] Sir Thomas Dale was Governor 1611 and 1614 to 1616. Sir Thomas
Gates as Governor organised the colony 1611 to 1614. See *Dictionary of
National Biography*, xxi. p. 64.

C

some Frenchmen introduced by Lord Delawarr. Even in England the affairs of the Company had changed for the better, as in 1612 a fresh charter had been obtained, by which the Bermudas or Somers Islands were added to its dominions.

Prosperous as the colony appeared there was ever the menace of the Indian tribes with whom an intermittent war had been waged for some time, and during which Powhattan had taken captive several of the settlers. Peace, however, existed between the English and Japazaus, the Indian chief of the district along the Potomac, to whom Samuel Argall was sent by the Governor to trade for corn. This was not Argall's first visit to Japazaus, and a certain friendship existed between the two, the Indian chief regarding himself as indebted to the Englishman. With the King of the Potomac district, as wife of one of his captains, was the romantic Pocahontas, daughter of Powhattan. To the unscrupulous and ready-witted Argall this appeared a glorious opportunity of demanding the Princess as a hostage, and paying off old scores against Powhattan. Argall broached the subject to Japazaus, who readily accepted the plan. The story is told with strict truth by Ralph Hamor, the secretary of the colony, who says, " Capt. Argall, having secretly well rewarded him, with a small copper kettle, and som other les valuable toies so highly by him esteemed, that doubtlesse he would have betraied his owne father for them, permitted both him and his wife to returne," [1] but Pocahontas remained a captive. Hearing of his daughter's plight Powhattan immediately restored some of his prisoners and

---

[1] Hamor, *A True Discourse of the Present Estate of Virginia* (ed. 1860).

demanded her surrender, but the English not being satisfied, asked for more.   By this time other influences were at work, and Pocahontas exhibited no desire to return to her people.   In the spring of 1613, she was baptised by the name of Rebecca, and married to one of the most influential settlers, John Rolfe, " a gentleman of approved behaviour and honest cariage." [1] The marriage was welcomed by the Indian chief, and peace was restored for the time being.   Pocahontas and her husband went to England in 1616, where she was fêted and presented at court, but the English climate did not suit the Indian beauty, and she died in the spring of the following year at Gravesend.

The year 1614 is memorable in Virginian history for the first hostile action between the English and their French rivals.   Samuel Argall, who has been classified as " a sea-captain with piratical tastes," attacked a French settlement on the coast of Maine and sacked Port Royal, the capital of Acadia or Nova Scotia.   These acts were contrary to all the principles of international law, but France, under the weak rule of Marie de' Medici, was in no state to avenge her wrongs, and the matter dropped after a formal complaint by the French ambassador.   This and other weighty questions caused an animated discussion in Parliament concerning the rights and privileges of Virginia.   Martin, the advocate of the Company, told the House to look to the advantages to be gained in Virginia, and not to waste their time on the trifles that generally engaged their attention.   In fact, his speech was so heated that he was forced to confess his errors

[1] Hamor, *A True Discourse of the Present Estate of Virginia* ed. 1860).

on bended knee, and with that the House of Commons was satisfied, and dropped the subject.

After the retirement of Gates, Sir Thomas Dale continued the government of Virginia under the merciless code ; and yet the colony prospered, private industry and private property being allowed. Dale's second period of office was for two years only, and he departed at a time when a greedy and unprincipled set of men began to administer the affairs of the Company. In 1617 they selected as their Deputy Governor in Virginia the most unsuitable Samuel Argall. Certainly he was a man endowed with ability and resolute courage, but he was one of the few unscrupulous villains who have disgraced colonial history. Immediately on coming into power he issued a series of edicts of arbitrary character. Trade with the Indians was forbidden, but this was not for the advantage of the shareholders of the Company, but for the benefit of their deputy. The settlers were made to work as slaves for Argall, for whom the constitution of the colony afforded splendid opportunities. Such a state of affairs was not to last for long ; the despotic conduct of the Governor leaked out at identically the moment the Company passed into the hands of a more honest and capable set of directors.[1] Sir Edwin Sandys, a leader of that party which was soon to turn boldly against the King, together with the brilliantly versatile Southampton and the skilled John Ferrars, were now at the head of Virginian affairs in England.

The history of Virginia changed for the better in 1619, when Sir George Yeardley superseded the

---

[1] The characters of the two parties is controversial owing to the scarcity of documentary evidence.

piratical Argall. The new Governor was not a particularly strong man, and in many of his actions he proved himself a weak successor of the stern Sir Thomas Dale. On the other hand there was beneath the somewhat too gentle exterior a man of considerable worth, for he succeeded in governing peaceably a turbulent people without falling back upon unnecessary severity. Yeardley's first year of administration is ever famous for the establishment of the earliest representative assembly in the New World. It is only natural that a fully developed scheme was not evolved at once. There is some uncertainty as to what classes actually obtained the franchise, but it is probable that every freeman possessed a vote. Certain it is, however, that each plantation and each county returned two members, and it is equally well-known that the assembly took upon itself both legislative rights and judicial powers. Thus the year 1619 witnessed the creation of Virginia as an almost independent power heralding a revolutionary change in the near future.

The colony seemed prosperous in every way, but there were dark clouds overshadowing the Company on all sides. It was rumoured, and with some truth, that five thousand emigrants had landed in Virginia, and yet only one thousand were actually resident. Men asked themselves the question, "had the settlers returned, or had they died in this so-called land of promise"? The new board of directors, if they had been left to themselves, would have put the Company upon an assured footing, and success would most certainly have attended their efforts. But this was not to be ; the Company was attacked from within and without. Lord Warwick's party, a clique within the

Company, showed every sign of hostility to Southampton and Sandys. The external attacks came from three sources, not the least important being that of the Crown. James I. was jealous of the power of that Company which he himself had created. His fears were increased by the insidious attacks of the Spanish ambassador, Gondomar, who informed the King that "a seditious Company was but the seminary to a seditious Parliament."[1] Even the English people, little realising the work that the Company was painfully accomplishing for Imperial purposes, now turned against the men whom, for sentimental reasons, they ought to have supported, and used the popular cry against monopolies to bring about the downfall of the founders of a new nation. The dangers of the Company were increased by the perils of the colony itself. The old Indian hostility had for a few years slumbered, but after the death of Powhattan and the succession of Opechancanough in 1618 the horrors of Indian warfare once more threatened the colony. In the following year the death of a famous Indian, Jack the Feather, was a sufficient pretext, and Opechaucanough attacked Virginia. The English proved successful in the end, but not before they had lost three hundred and seventy of their number. It is not to be wondered at that the Assembly issued a severe order that "the inhabitants of every plantation should fall upon their adjoining savages";[2] this the planters readily obeyed; and the steps taken, though harsh, appear to have been effectual.

The news of the Indian massacres, the action of Spain and the absurd desire of a Spanish marriage, worked upon the mind of James I. to such an extent

---

[1] Doyle, *op. cit.* p. 220.   [2] *Ibid.*, p. 226.

that he determined to abolish the Company.[1]   In 1623 the King demanded the surrender of the charter, which Sandys and his party stoutly refused.   A writ of *quo warranto* was then issued to decide whether the privileges of the Company were purely a monopoly, or whether they were exercised for the public good.   The Law Courts gave a verdict against the Company, and the charter was declared null and void.   The storm cloud, which had long hung over the Company, had now burst upon the heads of the devoted directors. They were forced to succumb to the most pernicious of all influences, for they had been crushed by greed and covetousness, together with the intrigues of disgraceful courtiers and disappointed speculators who showed a lack of public spirit that too often marked the early years of the Stuart period.   In reviewing the actions of the Company it is universally agreed that they had in almost every case been for good ; it is, however, acknowledged with similiar unanimity that for the actual benefit of the colony in the future it was as well that the Company's powers should pass to the Crown.   Had the actions of the Company been disliked in the colony itself, it is inexplicable that the colony should have supported the Company at the time of its trial.   The settlers could not foresee what might be the outcome of a continuance of the Company's rule.   At the time they merely realised with disgust that James had acted as he had done, solely to gain the fickle and grudging favour of the decadent Spain ; but they did not understand that the Company must inevitably in the future, if it had not already done so in the past, act as a trammelling influence upon the

---

[1] There was no question of abandoning the colony itself, which was what Spain desired.

progress and prosperity of the little settlement. Unwittingly James, by his action, had removed the fetters, and had given an opportunity of free growth to the colony. It was no longer possible for the welfare of the individual planter to be sacrificed to the merely temporary advantage of the English trader and share-holder. "Morally and politically, indeed, the abroga-tion of the Virginian charter was a crime"; but "the colony, happily for its future, passed under the control of the Crown while it was yet plastic, undeveloped and insignificant."[1] Henceforth the constitution of Virginia was of the normal type; the administration was carried on by a governor and two chambers, the one nominated, the other popularly elected.

The first chapter of Virginian history may be said to have closed when the Company ceased to exist, and at the same time the romantic and heroic aspect of the colony was concluded. Although perhaps no individual connected with the foundation of the colony can be compared with the glorious figures of the Elizabethan epoch, yet in the characters of Hakluyt, Southampton, Sandys, and Captain John Smith there was something of the old order. The heroism of the first actors upon the Virginian stage was probably as great as that of their predecessors, but the new order of things did not call upon them to exhibit such feats of strength or of bravery. By the abrogation of the Company's charter a revolution had indeed been effected. From this moment the history of Virginia can only be dealt with in a brief and hasty sketch, for happy is the country that has no history, and such is the case with regard to the later years of England's first great colony. The interests of the settlers are in the future mainly con-

[1] Doyle, *op. cit.* pp. 242, 244.

fined to the growth of tobacco, as will be shown in a later chapter, and from 1623 the chroniclers cease to record the story of the terrible struggle for bare existence, but tell rather the tale of a steady but unheroic prosperity amongst a rich class of planters employing negro labour.

The first Governor under the Crown was Sir Francis Wyatt, who was of good character and inspired the colonists with a self-reliant temper.   He was succeeded in 1626 by Sir George Yeardley, who had already won the affection of many of the settlers in the days of the Company's rule.   The following year, however, Yeardley died ; and the Crown appointed a creature of its own, Governor Harvey, who quarrelled with the Assembly on every possible occasion.   In fact so bitter did these quarrels become that a settler, Mathews by name, as leader of the popular party, seized Harvey in 1635, and placed him upon a vessel where he was kept in honourable confinement until the old country was reached.   It is hardly likely that the colonists imagined that the Crown would take their part against the Governor, but their action was probably due to a general desire to impress the Crown with their power. Charles I., who had previously shown good feeling towards the colony, now behaved foolishly in sending Harvey back to Virginia, where he remained for four years, filling up his time by sending numerous petty and querulous complaints to the home country of the misdoings of the settlers.   During Harvey's administration the old proprietors made several attempts to obtain a fresh grant of the charter and the reinstitution of the Company.   But with the same ardent spirit as the colonists had supported the Company in 1623, so now they opposed its re-establishment and for the same reason. The change that they had imagined must inevitably take place by the abolition of the Company was a loss of their titles ; but having been firmly settled under the Crown they were frightened that if the Company should be again created their titles would be again endangered. The advocate of the colonists was the pliant and pliable Sandys, who, when he reached England, deserted his constituents, and pleaded for the restoration of the old rule. The colony immediately on hearing of this sent word to the King that their representative was acting contrary to their wishes, and in 1639 they received the satisfactory reply that Charles had no intention of restoring the Company.

From this time the settlers appear from contemporary records to have been contented. The writers point out how nature gave freely, how beautiful was the land, and how peaceful were the natives. There can be no doubt that this was the content and boastfulness of a young people, and that it was unduly exaggerated. On the other hand it must also be allowed that though Virginia was not quite the paradise represented in some of the letters written by the settlers, yet it was, when the Civil War broke out in England, a land of comparative peace and plenty.

Sir Francis Wyatt was again sent out to succeed Governer Harvey in 1639, but his period of office was short and uneventful. More stirring times came when the colony passed under the rule of Sir William Berkeley. He was a typical cavalier, bluff in speech, hot in temper, brave in danger, and contemptuous of learning. He may, in later years, have exercised a merciless tyranny, but it was the hardship of his

fortunes together with something closely akin to
lunacy that drove him to such actions. On his
appointment, his instructions were more carefully
formulated than had hitherto been the case. This
was only natural as the Court party at home were
beginning to see the dangers that were looming a-head,
and so they trusted that in Virginia trouble might be
checked by the exaction of the strictest oaths of
allegiance and supremacy, and by the insistence on
the service of the Church of England. This latter
was hardly necessary as speaking widely the Church
of England was the Church of the Virginians. There
were, however, three parishes, the members of which
were almost entirely nonconformists until dispersed
and scattered by a conformity act between the years
1642 and 1644.

Sir William Berkeley had hardly taken up the reins
of government when the history of the colony was
marked by a great calamity. Opechancanough was
now an old man, enfeebled in body and physically
incapable of leading his people ; but his mind was
still as active as ever, his savage cunning was in no
way dimmed by years, and he had ever nursed the
hatred he had felt for the settlers since the failure of
his attack in the days of the Company. The rumours
of the outbreak of the Civil War in England soon
reached the ears of the Indians, some of whom had
actually seen two ships of the white settlers bombard-
ing each other in the Bay. Opechancanough seized
this opportunity of division and strife among the
Virginians, and fell upon the colony. Before the
settlers were ready to resist, three hundred men,
women and children had been slain. The local
militia at last made headway against the savages,

and after the capture and death of the old chief in
1646 a treaty was made as to the boundary between
the English and the Indians, under which peace
reigned for thirty years.

It has been the fashion to regard Virginia as a
purely Cavalier colony ; this is probably due to an
attempt to accentuate the difference between the
Southern colony and the New England group. It
is, however, an exaggeration to say that Virginia
was entirely composed of those supporting cavalier
principles. Certainly there were large landowners
who sympathised with Charles and his party, but
there was a very large and prosperous middle class,
composed of small landowners and well-to-do trades-
men, amongst whom it was only natural to find
various opinions and sympathies. As a whole, however, Virginia may be said to have been Royalist, not
from any rooted objection to the Commonwealth, but
rather because the Royalist party was temporarily
predominant in the settlement. Sir William Berkeley,
as a loyal Governor, forbade the showing of any
sympathy to the Parliamentary rebels, and he was
supported in his action by Charles II., who, in 1650,
before he left Breda, despatched a commission em-
powering Berkeley to act in his name. The far-
reaching power of Cromwell was not to be stayed by
any such commission, for the Commonwealth was
determined " to grasp the whole of the inheritance of
the Stuart Kings," [1] and so Ayscue was sent in 1651
to reduce the colonies to submission. On March 12
of the following year, Virginia acknowledged the new
power in England, much to the rage and discontent of
the Governor. Berkeley had indeed done his best,

---

[1] Gardiner, *History of the Commonwealth*, i. 317.

and had issued a stirring declaration which concluded
with these words, " But, gentlemen, by the Grace of
God we will not so tamely part with our King and
all those blessings we enjoy under him, and if they
oppose us, do but follow me, I will either lead you to
victory or lose a life which I cannot more gloriously
sacrifice than for my loyalty and your security." [1]
The settlers, however, were not stirred, and though a
thousand men had been collected at Jamestown, the
Assembly refused their support, not so much for the
love of Cromwell as because they feared material loss
if they resisted him.   Had the great Protector lived
longer the history of the American colonies might
have been very different.   He was the first Englishman who can really be said to have understood in its
fullest sense the word Empire.   But the gods were
not generous to this imperialist, and they did not
grant to him the necessary time for the achievement
of a policy which Cromwell himself classed as similar
to that of " Queen Elizabeth of famous memory." [2]
As it was, the rule of the Commonwealth had little
definite effect upon Virginia, except that it necessitated
a change in governors.   The first was Richard
Bennet, who was elected by the Assembly in 1652,
and ruled for three years.   His successor, Edward
Digges, was a worthy and sensible man, under whose
administration the colony continued a calm and happy
existence for one year.   In 1656 Samuel Mathews
was chosen, but during his rule Virginian history was
unimportant, and the only cloud upon the horizon
was an Indian panic which came to nothing.

The submission of Virginia was for the time only,

---

[1] Neill, *Virginia Carolorum* (1886), p. 215.
[2] *Cromwell's Speech V.*, Sept. 17, 1656.

and at the restoration of Charles II. once more the
royalist party became supreme.   The King was
accepted with perfect quiescence, and it is probable
that the Virginians, like the English, rejoiced at the
change, looking forward to the return of more mirthful
and joyous days.   As England learnt to repent the
return of the Stuarts, so also Virginia found that she
had fallen upon evil times, a fact which is partially
shown in Berkeley's report in 1671.   " As for the
boundaries of our land, it was once great, ten degrees
in latitude, but now it has pleased his Majesty to
confine us to halfe a degree.   Knowingly I speak
this.   Pray God it may be for his Majesty's service,
but I much fear the contrary. . . . I thank God,
there are *no free schools*, *nor printing*, and I hope we
shall not have these hundred years ; for *learning* has
brought disobedience, and heresy, and sects into the
world, and *printing* has divulged them, and libels
against the best government.   God keep us from
both." [1]

The greed of the cavaliers under Charles II. is
notorious, and it affected Virginia just as much as it
did England.   Lord Arlington and Lord Culpeper
obtained in 1672 the most monstrous rights, together
with a grant by which the whole soil of the colony
passed into their hands.   An agency was at once sent
to England to oppose this discreditable action, at the
same time taking with them a charter for which they
hoped to obtain ratification from the King.   Needless
to say in this they were unsuccessful ; but the charter
is historically important, because it contained a clause
stating that the colonists could not be taxed without
the consent of their own legislature.   The work of

[1] Hening, *Statutes at Large* (New York, 1823), ii. p. 517.

the agency partly failed owing to the supineness of Governor Berkeley ; chiefly, however, because the people of Virginia were unable to see that agencies could not be sent without expenditure. When a poll-tax was enacted to cover the necessary expenses of their agents, there was a popular outburst.

The inhabitants of Virginia at this time were much divided, and composed of distinct classes, the well-to-do planter, the tradesman, the " mean whites," the negro and the criminal. The last class had been growing steadily for some years as the colony had been used as a dumping-ground for gaol-birds, and indeed the criminal section would have increased still more had it not been for the better class of settlers who determined to stop it. In April 1670, the General Court held at Jamestown issued a notice " because by the great numbers of felons and other desperate villains being sent over from the prisons in England, the horror yet remaining of the barbarous designs of those villains in September 1663, who attempted at once the subversion of our religion, laws, liberties, rights and privileges," we do now prohibit " the landing of any jail-birds from and after the 20th of January next upon pain of being forced to carry them to some other country." [1] Although this law tended to exclude a cheap form of labour, nevertheless between 1669 and 1674 Virginia, commercially, was in a most flourishing condition, raising a greater revenue for the Crown than any other settlement. Sir John Knight informed Lord Shaftesbury that £150,000 in customs on tobacco alone had been paid, " so that Virginia is as of great importance to his Majesty as the Spanish Indies to Spain, and employs more ships and breeds more

[1] *Calendar of State Papers*, Colonial, 1669-1674, p. 64.

seamen for his Majesty's service than any other trade."[1]

Commercial success was not the only thing that went to make up Virginian history, for there were signs of external danger only too plainly exhibited by numerous outrages on the part of the Indians.   Had Berkeley shown any skill or energy in suppressing these disorders all might have gone well ; as it was he did nothing, with dire results.   The incapacity of the Governor at last aroused the wrath of a young, honest, courageous, but indiscreet, member of the Assembly, named Nathaniel Bacon.   He took up arms and was at first pardoned, but when he once again attempted to seize Jamestown he was taken, and died in so mysterious a manner as to give rise to rumours of poison and treachery, though it was also reported, " that, he dyed by inbibing or taking in two (*sic*) much Brandy."[2]   Bacon's rising had the effect desired in so far as it brought about the recall of Berkeley. So vindictively and cruelly did the Governor punish Bacon's followers that in 1677 the Crown sent three Commissioners, Sir John Berry, Colonel Francis Moryson, and Colonel Herbert Jeffreys to look into the grievances of either side.   They almost immediately quarrelled with the Governor, who was anxious to carry on his severe punishments.   The King, however, had commanded the Commissioners to show, if possible, the greatest lenience.   As a matter of fact out of a population of 15,000, only 500 were on the side of the Governor, and this small party who claimed to be the loyalists, very naturally advocated confiscations and fines.   Berkeley obstructed the Com-

[1] *Calendar of State Papers*, Colonial, 1669-1674, p. 530.
[2] *Strange News from Virginia* (1677), p. 8.

missioners as well as he was able, showing himself reckless of all consequences, and exhibiting gross discourtesy to the King's representatives. The truth was that Berkeley was growing old, and had possessed unlimited power far too long, supported as he had been by a most corrupt Assembly. The end of the quarrel came when the Governor, or more probably, Lady Berkeley, insulted the officials beyond forgiveness. After a consultation at the Governor's house the Commissioners were sent away in his carriage with "the common hangman" for postillion.[1] This outrage upon the laws of hospitality was too much; and Jeffreys immediately assumed the reins of government. Sir William Berkeley gave one more snarl, informing the new Governor that he was "utterly unacquainted"[2] with the laws, customs, and nature of the people; he then sailed for England, which he reached just alive, but "so unlikely to live that it had been very inhuman to have troubled him with any interrogations; so he died without any account given of his government."[3]

Sir Herbert Jeffreys had a difficult task before him in trying to purge the Assembly. Within a year of taking up office he died, leaving no lasting memorial of his skill as Governor, but he is "to be remembered as the first of a long series of officers of the standing army who have held the governorship of a colony."[4] Jeffreys' successor, Sir Henry Chicheley, only held office for a few months, and at his departure the old type of governor disappears. The year 1679 is remarkable for the new method of administration, a

[1] *Calendar of State Papers*, Colonial, 1677-1680, p. 64.
[2] *Ibid.*, p. 67.   [3] *Ibid.*, p. iv.
[4] Fortescue, *Introduction to Calendar*, 1677-1680, p. v.

D

method which proved injurious to the colony.
Thomas, Lord Culpeper, was the first of the new
scheme, and though he resided in the colony for four
years he did nothing for its inhabitants.   The appointment of Culpeper was most ill-advised, as he was
already detested owing to the grant of 1672.   He
took up his office at identically the same time as the
burgesses acquired the right of sitting as a separate
chamber, and he found the council refractory, the
colony unprosperous, and the Company of his
Majesty's Guards in "mutinous humours." [1]   His
tenure of office expired in 1684, and he was succeeded
by Lord Howard of Effingham.   It cannot be said
that the new Governor was idle, but whatever he did
was to the disadvantage of Virginia and the Virginians.
By a scandalous system of jobbery he inflicted
grievous financial injury upon individuals, and at the
same time retarded the progress of the colony by a
system of new imposts.   By his skill he obtained for
the Governor and the Council the right of appointing
the Secretary to the Assembly, which ought not to
have been allowed by a free representative body.
From this time the evils of the English colonial
system became apparent, and it is now that absentee
governors enrich themselves at the expense of their
settlements, the actual administration being left to
lieutenant governors in the confidence of their chiefs,
who remained at home.

The great stumbling-block to colonial prosperity
was the lack of unity between the different settlements
on the eastern coast of North America.   In 1684 an
attempt was made to bring about united action against
Indians, who had desolated the western borders of the

---

[1] *Calendar of State Papers*, Colonial, 1677-1680, p. 589.

English colonies. A conference was called at Albany, and Virginia, like all the other colonies, sent delegates to discuss the possibility of creating the United States under the British Crown. Nothing, however, came of it, for the jealousies and wranglings of the delegates only too well illustrated the feelings of the different settlements for each other. The Revolution of 1688 was accepted with tranquillity in Virginia, and two years later Francis Nicholson was appointed King William's lieutenant governor. Nicholson was a man of much colonial experience, of violent temper, and scandalous private life. He strongly opposed the desire for political freedom, but at the same time he made an excellent governor, and during his rule, which lasted until 1704 (except for a period of six years, 1692-1698), the colony prospered. A desire for education evinced itself at this period, and in 1691 Commissary Blair was sent to England to obtain a patent for the creation of a college. He returned within two years, his labours having been crowned with success, and in 1693 the second university [1] in America was established under the title of William and Mary College.

As the seventeenth century drew to a close, Virginian progress was stimulated by the settlement, on the upper waters of the James River, of De Richebourg's colony of Huguenots, which is said to have "infused a stream of pure and rich blood into Virginian society." If the test of a colony is its population, Virginia at this time must have been most flourishing. Less than a century had passed since Newport and his one hundred and forty-three settlers had sailed into the James River; the colony had

[1] See p. 93.

suffered privations, had witnessed many a fluctuation of fortune, but at the dawn of the eighteenth century about one hundred thousand souls were living there in peace, plenty and happiness.   During the century that had passed, the settlers had won for themselves political rights, and practically, political freedom. They were to a certain extent restricted by the Navigation Acts, but the influence of the Crown or of the English Parliament was hardly felt.   Their interest in English political life was meagre ; the importance of getting trustworthy lieutenant governors was far greater to the Virginian than whether Whig or Tory was in power at home.   Sometimes the colony was fortunate, sometimes the reverse, but in every case the lieutenant governor was opposed to any extension of political rights.   The difficulty of united effort on the part of the planters was, to a certain extent, intensified by a want of towns.   Hampton was Virginia's chief port, and was composed of a hundred poor houses, while Williamsburg cannot be regarded as a true centre of either economic or intellectual activity.   This lack of town life is pointed out by Commissary Blair, who informed the Bishop of London, " even when attempts have been made by the Assembly to erect towns they have been frustrated. Everyone wants the town near his own house, and the majority of the burgesses have never seen a town, and have no notion of any but a country life." [1]   The lieutenant governors during the eighteenth century had not only to contend with the supineness of the settlers, but also with intercolonial discord.   Thus Alexander Spotswood, in 1711, attempted to assist North Carolina against the Tuscarora Indians, but he

---

[1] *Calendar of State Papers*, Colonial, 1697, p. 642.

received no support from either the Council or Assembly of Virginia. Five years later Spotswood was met with similar bickerings and squabbles when South Carolina was invaded by the Yamassees. In 1741 Oglethorpe begged assistance to protect the newly established Georgia; instead of sending their best we are told that his officer brought back "all the scum of Virginia." [1]

The worst feature of Virginian life was the omnipresent and omnipotent slave system, but from the mere commercial aspect this was in favour of the colony at the time. The planters, however, were never ready to leave the colony for imperial purposes owing to the fear of a negro rising at home. This was one of the chief difficulties with which the Governor, Robert Dinwiddie, had to contend, during that trying period of French and Indian attack, which prepared the way for the Seven Years' war. With this period it is not proposed to deal now, but to leave it to a later chapter concerning the struggle between the French colonists in the north and west, and the English settlers upon the eastern sea-board during that period which is peculiarly connected with Britain's imperial story.

[1] *Itinerant Observations*, p. 62.

CHAPTER III

THE COLONISATION OF MARYLAND AND THE CAROLINAS

"MARYLAND is a province not commonly knowne in England, because the name of Virginia includes or clouds it, it is a Country wholy belonging to that honorable Gentleman the Lord Baltamore."[1] Such is the description of the colony that now comes before us, and at the time it was penned John Hammond, the writer, told the truth. The colony had arisen under rather peculiar circumstances, which neither resembled the foundation of Virginia nor the settlement of the Pilgrim Fathers. In 1632 Charles I. granted to George Calvert, first Lord Baltimore, an ill-defined tract of territory to the north of Virginia. Baltimore was an old hand at colonisation, for he had some years previous attempted to form a settlement in Newfoundland which had not been successful. David Kirke, who took over the Baltimore lands there, said that Newfoundland agreed with all God's creatures except Jesuits and schismatics, and that a great mortality among the former tribe had driven Baltimore away. Whether this was the true reason, or whether, as it has been proposed, Baltimore was practically driven out by the Presbyterians, it is hard to decide. His next trial as a

---

[1] Hammond, *Leah and Rachel* (London, 1656), p. 20.

colony founder was made in the more southern lands
of Virginia, but here his Roman Catholicism was
sternly opposed by the English Church party.   Under
these circumstances his Maryland colony seemed
likely to flourish, for there were neither schismatics
nor churchmen, nor Presbyterians, but only Indians
to contend against.   Before the first Lord Baltimore
could accomplish anything he died, but the grant was
transferred to his son Cecil.   The charter is an important one, for by it the Proprietors gained both
territorial and political rights ; the freemen or representative assembly were to be consulted, and with
their advice the Proprietor could enact laws.   All
places of worship were to be consecrated according
to the Church of England, and so the Roman Catholic
faith had only a subordinate position in a colony
which owed its foundation to a true upholder of that
belief.   From the very first Maryland was better off
than several of the other colonies, as the Crown
divested itself of the right of levying taxes within
the province; but in other respects the constitution
was normal, consisting of a governor and two chambers,
the proprietor possessing the privilege of creating
councillors.

Leonard Calvert, brother of the second Lord
Baltimore, sailed to take possession in 1633, accompanied by two Jesuit priests and three hundred
emigrants.   These colonists were neither gaol-birds
nor religious fanatics ; they had been selected with
great care and were well provided.   One of the Jesuits,
Father White, has left on record his *Impressions* in
which he says that the colony was founded with a
definite religious and educational purpose.   " We had
not come thither for the purpose of war, but for the

sake of benevolence, that we might imbue a rude race with the precepts of civilisation, and open up a way to heaven, as well as impart to them the advantages of remote regions."[1] When the settlers came to the place of landing they "beheld the natives armed. That night fires were kindled through the whole region, and since so large a ship had never been seen by them messengers were sent everywhere to announce 'that a canoe as large as an island had brought as many men as there was trees in the woods.'"[2] From this moment and onwards the relations with the natives were always friendly. The small independent landowners being free from this danger, at first, lived happy and contented lives, but they were gradually crushed out of existence by large estate-holders working with gangs of indentured labourers.

The people of Virginia looked with some scorn upon their modern neighbours, and it was not long before a quarrel took place. The Isle of Kent lay in such a position off the coast that under Baltimore's patent it ought to have been included in the province of Maryland. But in 1625 the Virginians had settled there for trading purposes, and were determined not to be brought under the yoke of Baltimore's proprietorship. Two years after the establishment of Maryland, the Isle of Kent was under the rule of William Clayborne, a strong Protestant, a contentious man, who was described by his enemies as "a pestilent enemie to the wel-faire of that province and the Lord Proprietor."[3]

Calvert, anxious to establish the rights of his

---

[1] White, *A Relation of the Colony of the Lord Baron Baltimore in Maryland* (ed. 1847).
[2] *Ibid.*   [3] Hammond, *ut supra.*

brother, sent two ships to the Isle of Kent, and these were attacked by the crew of a pinnace belonging to Clayborne, lives being lost on both sides. The quarrel continued with so much fervour that it became merged in the greater struggle of the Civil War. Calvert was granted by the King letters of marque for privateering purposes, and he took good care to prey upon his enemy, Clayborne, whose friend Ingle had been furnished with similar letters from Parliament. Thus having placed the quarrel which was really personal under the banners of King and Parliament, the two rivals contended with each other.

The Parliamentary forces were, at first, successful ; Ingle and Clayborne invaded Maryland, seized St Mary's, and Calvert was obliged to fly. But with assistance from Governor Berkeley of Virginia, he returned and drove out the Clayborne faction which had disgusted the people by its incapacity and greed. The quarrel ceased for a short time, owing to Calvert's death ; but it was not long before it was renewed. Lord Baltimore appointed as his deputy William Stone, an ardent nonconformist and Parliamentarian, who repaid the Proprietor's generosity by leaguing with the people of the Isle of Kent. Traitor though he was, it is to be remembered that during his period of rule one good act was passed. Maryland was already celebrated for its toleration, but in 1649 it was still further enacted that a christian was not to be " in any ways molested or discountenanced for or in respect of his or her religion, nor in the free exercise thereof." [1]

For the peace of their minds and the preservation of their property Stone and the settlers acknowledged

[1] Bozman, *History of Maryland*, 1633-60 (1837), vol. ii. p. 661.

the Parliamentary commissioners, including Clayborne, who landed in 1652. They first displaced Stone, but realising that he was popular, and thinking that it would be advantageous for them, reinstated him. Stone, however, once more proved a trimmer, and sided with the Proprietor ; his late followers deserted him and turned to Clayborne. On the establishment of the Protectorate in 1654 Lord Baltimore asserted his rights, claiming that he now held from the Protector Cromwell, and declaring that the commissioners' privileges had ceased. Clayborne and his companions were not the men to take such a rebuff as this. " It was not religion, it was not punctilios they stood upon, it was that sweete, that rich, that large country they aimed at." [1] With this desire, according to a contemporary, Clayborne asserted his authority by disfranchising the Roman Catholics and forbidding the oath of loyalty to the Proprietor. William Stone, stung to resistance and filled with importance as the representative of Lord Baltimore, took up arms and was defeated by the Protestant party at Providence in 1655. Many of Stone's followers were executed, and their property confiscated ; Stone himself was sentenced to death, but was reprieved. Clayborne's party now seemed triumphant, but the home authorities refused to bestow upon him the Isle of Kent, and within two years the Protector restored to Baltimore his proprietorship of Maryland. Trouble still continued, and in 1659 Josias Fendall, the Proprietor's Governor, so worked upon the members of Assembly that they claimed full legislative rights and complete independence of the Baltimore family.

[1] Hammond, *ut supra.*

At the Restoration the quarrel came to an end, and Lord Baltimore re-established his rights with nothing more than a mere show of force. Philip Carteret was appointed Governor, and during his term of office a mint was set up in the colony. He was succeeded in 1662 by Charles Calvert to the alarm of the Protestant inhabitants, who sent an extraordinary document to the Lord Mayor and London merchants entitled, " *Complaint from heaven with a hue and cry and a petition out of Virginia and Maryland, to the King and his Parliament against the Barklian and Baltimore parties. The platform is Pope Jesuit determined to overthrow England with fire and sword and destructions, and the Maryland Papists to drive us Protestants to purgatory.*" [1]   These, however, were purely imaginary troubles, and a more real one fell upon both Virginia and Maryland on August 27, 1667, when a terrific gale destroyed in two hours four-fifths of their tobacco and corn, and blew down 15,000 houses. On the whole Virginia suffered perhaps more than Maryland, but neither colony was really subject to such perils ; and both, during the first fifteen years of Charles II.'s reign, enriched themselves as well as the Proprietor or the Crown by the fertility of their soil. This period of prosperity, however, gave way to one of unrest.

By the death of Cecil, Lord Baltimore in 1675, Charles Calvert, the late Governor, succeeded as heir to the family titles, estates and proprietorship of Maryland, the latter being placed under his deputy, Thomas Notley. The Proprietor was not at first upon the best of terms with the home government. He was severely reprimanded by the Privy Council

---

[1] *Calender of State Papers*, Colonial, 1661-1668, p. 119.

for the imprisonment and assassination of a collector
of customs.   It is not hinted that Baltimore had any
actual hand in this crime, but it is thought that he
connived " at least *ex post facto* in his murder."   No
sooner had the Proprietor got over this difficulty, than
he fell out with the settlers, who were caused much
uneasiness in 1681 by the limitation of the franchise
to those freeholders of 50 acres or those owners of
other property of the value of £40.   A spirit of
unrest was therefore abroad, and there were not
wanting those who were ready to snatch the opportunity and pose as patriots against the aggression of
the Proprietor.   Josias Fendall, who had already
tried to deprive the Baltimore family of their rights,
and who had now become an unworthy demagogue,
leagued with John Coode, a clergyman, and revolted.
The insurrection, as such, was short-lived.   But exciting events were taking place in England, and Coode
again seized his chance when news of the Revolution
of 1688 drifted across the Atlantic.   He placed
himself at the head of the Association for the Defence
of the Protestant Religion, and in 1689, pretending
that he was serving William III., seized in the King's
name the government of Maryland.   The King
bestowed some signs of favour upon this clever
rebel, but his designs were soon discovered, and
the government of Maryland was radically changed.
In 1691 the colony was placed under the direct
control of the Crown ; the political rights of the
Proprietor were annulled ; the Church of England
was established, and the Roman Catholics were
persecuted.

The first royal Governor was Francis Nicholson,
who had served elsewhere successfully, but was

regarded with suspicion and dislike by many of the inhabitants of Maryland. Gerald Slye's accusations against Nicholson, in May 1698, give some idea of this dislike, and are of some interest as an indication of the means used by an ignorant colonist to discredit the Governor in England. A few of the accusations will show how utterly foolish these complaints were. Slye began by asserting that "all thinking men are amazed that such a man should have twisted himself into any post in the government, for besides his incapacity and illiteracy, he is a man who first in New York, then in Virginia, and at last in Maryland, has always professed himself an enemy to the present King and government." The next charge was that the Governor "makes his chaplain walk bareheaded before him from home to church." This is further extended by the fact that he "usually makes his chaplain wait ten or twelve hours for service so that often morning prayer is said in the evening." But there are more charges concerning Nicholson's treatment of his chaplain, for he, "a pious and good gentleman, the credit of the clergy in this province, happening one day by the Governor's means [to be] a little disguised in drink"[1] was suddenly summoned to conduct Divine Service. And so charge after charge of the same absurd character were brought against Nicholson not so much because of his ill-doing, but because he had the misfortune to be Governor.

The people of Maryland were not content until in 1715 the fourth Lord Baltimore became a Protestant, and by his conversion it was held that his full rights had revived. Fourteen years later the

---

[1] *Calendar of State Papers*, Colonial, 1697-1698, p. 246.

Proprietor's title obtained an everlasting memorial in the foundation of the city of Baltimore as a port for the planters.   The restoration of the Calverts to their former rights was by no means advantageous to the religious life of the colony.   The fourth lord was a hanger-on of Frederick, Prince of Wales, while the fifth to hold the title was a notorious profligate. These men insisted on exercising their right of clerical patronage without any regard to the welfare of the Church.   Thus George Whitefield, who visited the colony in 1739, failed to arouse religious fervour. His preaching in Maryland was far less successful than it had been in Virginia.   The former colony he found in " a dead sleep," and to use his own words, he " spoke home to some ladies concerning the vanity of their false politeness, but, alas ! they are wedded to their quadrille and ombre." [1]

If the Marylanders were conspicuous for their irreligion, they were equally noticeable for their industry.   A large number of German emigrants had come to the colony, and had started a continuous movement of extension towards the West.   To these Germans is entirely due the improved state of the country, and the better means of communication even beyond the mountains.   But the rolling westward of the Maryland population brought the colony into close touch with the power of France ; and like the other colonies it was destined, about the middle of the eighteenth century, to contend against the policy of the French King, by which, if it had been successful, the seaboard colonies would have been deprived of the possibility of further expansion towards the Pacific.

[1] *Letters*, vol. i. p. 135.

The history of the Carolinas only resembles that of Maryland in the fact that they were both proprietary colonies. The swampy and low-lying coast to the south of Virginia had, in the early years of colonisation, offered little temptation to settlers, and long remained uninhabited by Englishmen or Spaniards. Certainly in 1564, Laudonnière, a Huguenot gentleman and naval officer, attempted a plantation at Port Royal in South Carolina, and named his fortress Caroline, " in honour of our Prince, King Charles " ; [1] but it was an absolute failure, and the history of the fate of these Huguenots at the hands of the brutal Spaniard, Menendez, is as well-known as the tremendous retribution which followed his barbarous cruelty. Captains Amidas and Barlow, in 1584, at the charge and direction of Sir Walter Raleigh, visited this portion of the North American continent, but nothing came of it, and " Caroline " was left strictly alone as if a curse were upon the land. Adventurers from Virginia at last broke down the old prejudices, and by the year 1625 landseekers and discoverers had penetrated as far south as the Chowan. By a strange chance the country named by Laudonnière was destined in 1629 to receive much the same name from an Englishman for much the same reason. In that year Sir Robert Heath obtained from Charles I. a grant of land to the south of Virginia, which was called after the King "the province of Carolina." No practical result, however, came from this grant, and Carolina, as it may now be called, still remained uninhabited except for the natives.

The first real charter to the Lords Proprietor of Carolina was dated the 24th March 1663, but owing

[1] *Hakluyt's voyages* (edit. 1904), vol. ix. p. 17.

to the previous grant of Charles I. numerous legal steps had to be taken before matters were satisfactorily arranged.   The land between Virginia and Florida was now granted to eight patentees, amongst whom were the Duke of Albemarle, the Earl of Clarendon, Sir William Berkeley, but above all the Earl of Shaftesbury. These Proprietors had political and territorial authority, but there was also to be an assembly of freeholders with legislative powers.   Twenty thousand acres of land were reserved for the original Proprietors, but at the same time a notice was issued inviting planters to settle in the colony, promising one hundred acres to each settler within five years, together with the privilege of residing in a land blest with the doctrine of freedom of conscience.   This notice was published not only in England, but also in Barbadoes, the Bermudas, Virginia and New England, so that the colonisation of the Carolinas was not only, nor even mainly, undertaken by adventurers from the home country.   On Albemarle River a settlement was made from Virginia, which formed the nucleus of North Carolina.   Near Cape Fear the New Englanders also had a little colony which was absorbed by a more prosperous settlement from Virginia.   Settlers soon came from Barbadoes, for there the news had been welcomed, and hundreds of experienced planters showed themselves willing to accept the offer of the Proprietors, and expressed a desire to come with their negroes and servants. They had, no doubt, been tempted by the extra inducements published in August 1663, when the Carolinas were advertised as wonderfully healthy and a land capable of bearing commodities not yet produced in other plantations as wine, oil, currants, raisins, silks, etc.   Most of the Barbadoes planters were afterwards absorbed in the colony sent out from England forming the nucleus of South Carolina.

The history of the first year in the Carolinas is practically unknown, except that in September the province was divided into two, and the northern section seems to have been already settled. The growth of the colony must have been steady, for in June 1665, Thomas Woodward, surveyor for the Proprietors in Albemarle county, shows that the population has increased, and that "the bounds of the county of Albemarle, fortie miles square, will not comprehend the inhabitants there already seated."[1] He continues to give the Proprietors excellent advice, and recommends that they should show generosity if they wish to encourage settlers; "so if your Lordships please to give large Incouragement for some time till the country be more fully Peopled your Honore may contract for the future upon what condition you please. But for the present, To thenke that any men will remove from Virginia upon harder Conditione then they can live there will prove (I feare) a vaine Imagination, It bein Land only that they come for."[2]   There were however, others who continued to praise the colony, and one writer in 1670 says of Ashley River, "it is like a bowling alley, full of dainty brooks and rivers of running water; full of large and stately timber."[3] The reader can hardly refrain from wondering where the resemblance to a bowling alley is to be found. Again the panegyrist says in a somewhat peculiar sentence, "as of the land of Canaan, it may be said it is

[1] Saunders, editor of *Colonial Records of North Carolina*, p. 99.
[2] *Ibid.*, p. 100.
[3] *Calendar of State Papers*, Colonial, 1669-1674, p. 186.

E

a land flowing with milk and honey, and it lies in the same latitude." [1]   The Proprietors were very anxious to preserve this lovely land for the "better folk," and in December 1671 Lord Ashley wrote to Captain Holstead not to invite the poorer sort to Carolina, " for we find ourselves mightily mistaken in endeavouring to get a great number of poor people there, it being substantial men and their families that must make the plantation which will stock the country with negroes, cattle, and other necessaries, whereas others rely and eat upon us." [2]

Carolina's presiding genius and champion was Lord Shaftesbury's medical adviser, secretary, and personal friend, John Locke.   He is supposed in 1667 to have drawn up the Fundamental Constitutions which contained an elaborate scheme of feudal government.   Whether he did produce this astounding document has never been conclusively proved, nor is it of much value, since the principles contained in it were never enforced as a working system, for they were neither adapted to the times nor the conditions of a colony of freemen.   By the year 1670 the elective Assembly possessed the definite powers of appointing officers, establishing law courts, and superintending the military defences of the colony. These privileges did not prevent them committing a great blunder by which the colony was converted into a paradise for the bankrupt and the pauper, but a hell for the honest and willing settler.   It was now enacted that no colonist for the first five years after the true foundation of the colony should be liable for any exterior debts ;   that

---

[1] *Calendar of State Papers*, Colonial, 1669-1674, p. 187.
[2] *Ibid.*, p. 297.

no newcomer need pay any taxes for his first
year ; and that marriage should be regarded as
valid if mutual consent should be declared before the
governor.

The northern section of the colony suffered most,
and for fifty years this part of Carolina was wearied
by ever recurring disputes and insurrections. " The
colony indeed seems to have reached that chronic
state of anarchy when the imprisonment and deposition of a governor is a passing incident which hardly
influences the life of the community." [1]   Thus during
the government of Thomas Eastchurch, who was sent
out by the Proprietors to Albemarle in 1677, there
was much trouble.   Eastchurch appointed as his deputy
the immoral Thomas Miller of the King's Customs.
" Now Miller had a failing, not as the Proprietors point
out, the common one of religious bigotry which had
bred such dissension in New England, but a weakness
for strong liquor." [2]   On his arrival he undertook to
model the Parliament, " no doubt with alcoholic readi-
ness and assurance, which proceeding we learn without surprise gave the people occasion to oppose and
imprison him." [3]   Thereupon certain unscrupulous
men took Miller's place and began at once to collect
the Customs and so defrauded the Crown.   For some
short time angry words passed between the home
Government and the colony, but the storm was calmed
by the restoration of the King's duties.   Eastchurch
was succeeded by Culpepper, who controlled affairs
until Seth Sothel came out as governor in 1683.
The new ruler's rapacity and arbitrary conduct

---

[1] Doyle, *Cambridge Modern History* (1905), vol. vii. p. 35.
[2] Fortescue, *Calendar of State Papers*, Colonial, 1677-1680, p. ix.
[3] *Ibid.*, p. ix.

caused the Assembly to depose and banish him, paying no attention to the feeble remonstrance of the Proprietors.

Meanwhile the southern portion of Carolina, particularly the settlements of Yeamans at Cape Fear and Sayle at Charleston, proved themselves more orderly and promising than the anarchic Albemarle ; and probably for this reason the Proprietors displayed towards them more consideration. The constitution which was granted to Charleston in 1670 was most liberal in character, for not only were the freemen allowed to elect the members of the House of Representatives, but they also possessed the privilege of nominating ten out of the twenty councillors.   As so many of the settlers had come from Antiqua, "weary of the hurricane," [1] or from Barbadoes, they naturally reproduced their old methods of life, and having been accustomed to slaves, they tried to force the Indians into servility ; but they found the Red Indian very different from the African negro, for he was possessed of a proud spirit and remarkable cunning that saved him from serfdom. The community of the South was one of wealthy traders who generally lived in the capital, partly because of the fine harbour and the insalubrious swamps inland, and partly because of the scheme of the Proprietors by which every freeholder had a town lot one-twentieth the extent of his whole domain.

The first governor was William Sayle, of Barbadoes, described in 1670 as "a man of no great sufficiency." [2] It is very difficult at this distance of time to deduce the character of this governor, for Henry Brayne wrote,

---

[1] *Calendar of State Papers*, Colonial, 1669-1674, p. 620.
[2] *Ibid.*, p. 130.

"Sayle is one of the unfittest men in the world for
his place " ; and he then proceeded to call him " crazy."[1]
On the other hand, when Sayle died in 1671, being at
least eighty years of age, he is called " the good aged
governor " ;[2] and the Council of Ashley River, on
March 4, 1671, recorded that he was " very much
lamented by our people, whose life was as dear to
them as the hopes of their prosperity."[3]   Sayle's chief
work during his short period of office was an attempt
to inculcate godly ways amongst the somewhat un-
godly colonists.   He urged the Proprietors to send
out an orthodox minister, and proposed the man
" which I and many others have lived under as the
greatest of our mercies."[4]   He knew very well that
some special inducement would have to be held out
to the Proprietors, and so uses the scriptural words,
" for where the Ark of God is, there is peace and
tranquillity."[5]

Sayle was succeeded by Joseph West as governor
in 1671, but his appointment was only temporary, as
Lord Shaftesbury in the autumn of that year sent a
commission to Sir John Yeamans.   His unpopularity,
however, caused his deposition ; and Joseph West was
again nominated as governor in 1674, a post which
he filled with conspicuous satisfaction and success for
eleven years.   While West was still in office, the
Lords Proprietor issued an order in December 1679
for the proper establishment of Charlestown.   " Where-
fore we think fit to let you know that the Oyster
Point is the place we do appoint for the port-town, of
which you are to take notice and call it Charlestown,

---

[1] *Calendar of State Papers*, Colonial, 1669-1674, p. 137.
[2] *Ibid.*, p. 187.   [3] *Ibid.*, p. 169.
[4] *Ibid.*, p. 70.   [5] *Ibid.*, p. 86.

and order the meetings of the Council to be there
held, and the Secretary's, Registrar's, and Surveyor's
offices to be kept within that town.   And you are to
take care to lay out the streets broad and in straight
lines, and that in your grant of town-lots you do
bound everyone's land towards the streets in an even
line, and suffer no one to encroach with his buildings
upon the streets, whereby to make them narrower
than they were first designed."[1]   Such was the town
to which West welcomed the Huguenots who were
excluded from the colonies of their own country.
The Proprietors, too, appreciating the wisdom of their
governor, afforded the unhappy French means of
cultivating their native produce of wine, oil, and silk,
so that they soon established new homes for their
distressed brethren, " who return daily into Babylon for
want of such a haven."[2]   By the end of West's administration the Clarendon settlements centering round
Charlestown had become extremely well-to-do, and the
town government, which was of excellent character,
administered the affairs of about three thousand people.
But the southern territory fell into the evil ways of
North Carolina ; and after West's retirement, which
finally took place in 1685, a series of unsatisfactory
governors caused a continual bickering, ill-feeling, and
well nigh insurrection.   Sothel, whose bad government
in Albemarle was already known in the south, was
appointed governor in 1690 ; but after a year the
southern settlers, taking example from their northern
brethren, drove him out.

The Proprietors at last found that they had had
enough of this disgusting incompetence and anarchy.

---

[1] *Calendar of State Papers*, Colonial, 1677-1680, p. 455.
[2] *Ibid.*, p. xi.

The Locke Constitutions had failed in every way ; a change must be made ; and it appeared that an amalgamation of North and South under one governor might have the effect desired. Their first choice of an administrator was most unsuccessful; Philip Ludwell of Virginia found he had a hard task before him in restoring peace out of chaos and anarchy. The task was too much for him, and having proved himself incapable was succeeded by a Carolina planter, Thomas Smith, in 1692. Bickering and quarrels continued ; Indian attacks were occasionally met and dealt with ; but the southern Spaniards were an ever present danger that made Smith's rule no sinecure. After three years Joseph Archdale, a quaker, and one of the Proprietors, came out as governor, but after a few months in the colony he was succeeded by his nephew, Joseph Blake. The benign rule of both these governors gave at last to the Carolinas a peace which they had not known for twenty years. The Huguenots were once again welcomed by Blake, and although they had been steadily settling in the Carolinas, particularly since the Revocation of the Edict of Nantes in 1685, yet they now obtained a more hearty welcome and complete toleration. So much had Blake's government done for the Carolinas that the royal special agent in 1699 records, " if this place were duly encouraged, it would be the most useful to the Crown of all the Plantations upon the continent of America."

There were, however, two external dangers to which the Carolinas were exposed at the very moment they seemed to have obtained internal peace. The first was the new French settlement on the Mississippi ; the second was the fear of Spanish aggression from Florida. The French danger was never really very extreme, and the Carolinas escaped many of the horrors of New England history. But the Spanish peril was true enough, for as early as 1680 a party of Scotch Presbyterians were routed from their little settlement at Port Royal, and this was regarded by the Carolina settlers as a just cause of complaint and an insult to his Majesty King Charles. To their great disappointment in 1699, when Edward Randolph was sent out to make investigations concerning Spanish intrusions, he brought with him no troops for their protection. At the beginning of the eighteenth century, therefore, it appeared best to the settlers that for their own defence they should take offensive action.

The war of the Spanish Succession, or, as it was called in the colonies, Queen Anne's war, had broken out, and rumours had reached the settlers of a coming Spanish onslaught. To meet this, James Moore, a political adventurer, but a very brave and capable man, led 500 English and 800 Indian allies into Spanish territory and took the unprotected town of St Augustine; but the fort, which was used as a last stronghold, resisted him for three months, and as he was unprovided with siege guns, he was obliged to retire on the appearance of a Spanish man-of-war. Nothing daunted, but rather elated with their previous success, a larger raid was made in 1704. Sir Nathaniel Johnstone was now governor, and he commissioned Colonel Moore to attack Apalachee, eighty miles to the west of St Augustine. In this action Moore was again successful, as Colonel Brewton records that "by this conquest of Apalachee the Province was freed from any danger from that part during the whole war." [1]   The Spaniards, however, did not remain idle, and in 1706, in alliance with the French from Martinique, with a fleet of ten sail and a force of 800 men attacked Charlestown.   The inhabitants were terrified, and their anguish was intensified by the horror of a severe outbreak of yellow fever.   Many of them, therefore, fled from the town, but Sir Nathaniel Johnstone routed the combined forces of France and Spain and captured no fewer than 230 prisoners.

Factious quarrels within the Province itself now threatened the safety of the settlers.   Since 1691 North and South Carolina had been united under one governor, but the custom had been established that the northern portion of the colony was always under the administration of a deputy.   In 1711 Thomas Cary disputed with Edward Hyde as to which held the office ; it was decided in favour of the latter.   The purely personal quarrel drove Cary to forget his feelings of patriotism, and flying from Carolina he stirred up the Tuscarora Indians, who, with fiendish delight, attacked a small settlement of Germans from the Palatinate.   South Carolina, where the supreme governor dwelt, immediately dispatched an army to the assistance of the North, with the effect that apparent peace was gained and the army was no longer required.   Immediately upon its withdrawal, however, the Tuscaroras again fell upon the helpless people ; this was too much, vengeance must be taken ; and this fierce Indian tribe was practically decimated and forced to migrate north.

Although the Treaty of Utrecht was signed in 1713, and the Spanish War of Succession came to an end, yet there was little hope of peace in the West as long

[1] *Historical Collections of South Carolina* (New York, 1836).

as either side allied with the Indians. The fate of the Tuscaroras may have stimulated the Yamassee Indians to revenge in 1716. In April, headed by Spaniards, they massacred about eighty inhabitants of Granville County, South Carolina. Charles Craven, the governor, proved himself a man of vigour, activity, and stern resolve, and by his efforts within a few months the colony was assured of safety, and there was apparent peace between the settlers of Carolina and the Spaniards of Florida.

In the winter of 1719 that perpetual love of dissension, and dislike of any federal action, was once more manifested by the Assembly of South Carolina. The governor was a son of Sir Nathaniel Johnstone, and he had done his best for the Proprietors, but unlike the northern portions the South now disowned all proprietary rule and elected a governor under the Crown. The home authorities immediately sent out Francis Nicholson, a capable colonial official who had already had experience in New York, Virginia, and Maryland. Ten years later the Proprietors accepted the inevitable, and being compensated financially, handed over the Carolinas to the Crown. They probably never regretted the bargain, as in 1739 the war against Spain once more jeopardised the existence of the English settlements in the south, the inhabitants of which were in chronic fear of murder and rapine. The chief Spanish attack was made in 1742, when an army of 5000 landed at St Simon's, owing to the failure of Captain Hardy to intercept the enemy's fleet. The expedition was unsuccessful; the colonists held their own; eighty prisoners were brought into Charlestown; and the Spaniards retired.

The share taken by the two Carolinas in American history during the next few years was far less than that of other colonies, but will be dealt with in another chapter. The great interest of the early history of the Carolinas is that the colony won for itself against very considerable odds the rights of local government and freedom from the shackles of the Proprietors. The settlers exhibited from first to last that full determination which is peculiarly associated with those of English stock to control their own destiny without the leading-strings of a few, perhaps benevolent, but generally misguided, human beings, whose powers have been conferred upon them by chance. The settlers of the Carolinas were a dogged type of men who faced external dangers with courage and good sense, distinctly contradictory of their pig-headed, factious, anarchic spirit in all internal affairs.

CHAPTER IV

THE PURITANS IN PLYMOUTH AND MASSACHUSETTS

IT has been customary to regard the members of the colony of Virginia as Cavaliers of the most ardent type, but, as has been shown, this is scarcely correct, and amongst the Virginians there were many who did not approve of either the actions of Laud or the dissimulation of Charles. In much the same way it would be erroneous to ascribe to the New England group a plebeian origin. The Virginian gentleman found his counterpart in the New England colonies of Plymouth and Massachusetts. It is, however, more true to describe these two colonies as the offspring and embodiment of Puritanism, than to describe Virginia as purely monarchical. In the northern colonies, congregationalism was the chief form of religious worship, and this, as was natural, determined their political form ; it was no insurmountable step from a belief in congregations to a belief in republics. The men who found this step so easy were a very different pattern to the early ne'er-do-wells of Virginian colonisation. The northern colonies were founded by the yeoman and the trader, both of whom were patient, watchful, and ready to assert with an Englishman's doggedness all political rights. These men formed small organic communities filled with the very strongest sense of corporate life. Not that these forms took an absolutely exact line, for in some cases the community was a pure democracy with limitations and restrictions ; in others there was a very wide and modified oligarchy. The men were the very best of settlers ; they knew what they wanted, and were ready to work and even sacrifice their lives to gain that object. It is not surprising that in the New England colonies prosperity raised its head long before it had come to Virginia, though the soil of the latter was far more fertile than the sterile lands of the northern group.

The Plymouth Company had been formed at the same time as the London Company, but it had accomplished very little.[1] In 1607 it dispatched an expedition under George Popham and Raleigh Gilbert to the River Kennebec, in the territory afterwards called Maine. The climate, however, did not suit the adventurers, and owing to the mismanagement of the leaders and the indifference of the Company nothing came of the undertaking. For thirteen years the Plymouth Company made no further effort, but in 1620 it was entirely reorganised, placed upon a new footing, and renamed the New England Company. This may have been caused by two things. In the first place Captain John Smith had made a voyage to New England in 1614 ; it was indeed that resourceful but perhaps boastful adventurer who either gave the name by which the country was afterwards known, or gave currency to an already existing though not generally accepted title. " In the moneth of Aprill, 1614 . . . I chanced to arrive in *New-England*, a parte of *Ameryca* at the *Ile of Monahiggin*, in 43½ of

[1] See p. 24.

Northerly Latitude." [1]   But even this voyage and the several others that followed would not have been sufficient to arouse the Plymouth Company.   It was in truth a second and deeper cause that started the reorganisation of a corporation that had so long lain dormant.   A new force had now entered into colonisation that was to do much for the establishment of the Anglo-Saxon race in America.   Religion had sent men to convert the savages, but now religious persecution sent men to make homes amongst those barbarians.

It is unnecessary here to discuss the rise of the Puritans as an important sect in English history. They were those " whose minds had derived a peculiar character from the daily contemplation of superior beings and eternal interests." [2]   They differed in nearly every respect from the ordinary Englishman of the Elizabethan period, and yet they were in many instances intellectual and well-bred.   They saw, however, that " they could not have the Word freely preached and the sacraments administered without idolatrous gear," and so they concluded to break away from the Church.   It was this separation that gained for them the name of Separatists, and brought upon them the punishment of the State.   To avoid this some sought leave from Elizabeth to settle in the land " which lieth to the west," their object being to " settle in Canada and greatly annoy the bloody and persecuting Spaniard in the Bay of Mexico." [3]   Such was the knowledge of geography about 1591, and it was very fortunate for the would-be-colonists that

---

[1] Smith, *A Description of New England* (1616), p. 1.

[2] Macaulay, *Essays* (ed. 1891), p. 23.

[3] *Calendar of Domestic State Papers*, 1591-1594, p. 400.

nothing came of the scheme. Two years later some Independents of London fled to Amsterdam, where they hoped to exercise their religion unmolested. Soon after the beginning of the seventeenth century the Nonconformists of Gainsborough took refuge in the Low Countries, to be followed in 1606 by the Congregationalists from Scrooby. They first found shelter in Amsterdam, and later, some, choosing John Robinson as their minister, moved to Leyden.

The laws of England had driven these men abroad, but they never forgot the fact that they were Englishmen. They found their families growing up around them and naturally imbibing foreign ideas. This fact deeply pained the parents, who looked back upon their own happy youths in Tudor England. They determined, therefore, to leave the Netherlands, and William Bradford, their faithful chronicler, tells in quaint but honest words why they were driven to this decision. " In ye agitation of their thoughts, and much discours of things hear aboute ; at length they began to incline to this new conclusion, of remooual to some other place. Not out of any new fanglednes, or other such like giddie humor, by which men are oftentimes transported to their great hurt & danger. But for sundrie weightie & solid reasons." [1] The most serious of these reasons " and of all sorowes most heauie to be borne ; was that many of their children, by these occasions (and ye great licentiousnes of youth in y^t countrie) and ye manifold Temptations of the place, were drawne away by euill examples into extrauagante & dangerous courses, getting ye raines off their neks & departing from

[1] Bradford, *History of the Plimoth Plantation*, p. 15.

their parents.   Some became souldjers, others took vpon them farr viages by Sea ; and other some worse courses . . . so that they saw their posteritie would be in danger to degenerate & be corrupted." [1]   It was for this reason, then, in particular, that the people of the congregation of Leyden turned their thoughts to the " countries of America which are frutful & fitt for habitation ; being deuoyed of all ciuill Inhabitants ; wher ther are only saluage & brutish men which range vp and downe, litle otherwise than ye wild beasts of the same." [2]   And yet though they sought a home for themselves where they might worship as they pleased, they were at the same time filled with that missionary spirit which had encouraged Columbus and many another adventurer to persevere. Their great aim was to lay " some good foundation or at least make some way thereunto, for ye propagating & advancing ye gospell of ye Kingdom of Christ in those remote parts of ye world ; yea, though they should be but even as stepping stones unto others for ye performing of so great a work." [3]

With these intentions the ever famous Pilgrim Fathers came to England, bringing with them a document admitting the supremacy of the State in religious matters.   The wording of the clauses, however, was so artful that these Puritans proved that though gentle as doves they were not without the wisdom of the serpent.   They obtained leave from James I. to set out on their voyage ; but they were financed by certain London traders who were to receive all the profits for the first seven years, when the partnership was to be dissolved.   Until this dissolution the whole

---

[1] Bradford, *History of the Plimoth Plantation*, p. 16.
[2] *Ibid.*, p. 17.   [3] *Ibid.*

band was to live as a community with joint property, trade, and labour. A few labourers were sent out by the London partners, but the group to which the term of Pilgrim Fathers strictly applies was composed of forty-one Puritan emigrants and their families, who had, as a friend said, "been instrumental to break the ice for others ; the honours shall be yours to the world's end."[1] The voyage of the *Mayflower* is now one of the most familiar events in the history of the British Empire. The little vessel, accompanied by the *Speedwell*, which had to return, sailed from Plymouth in August 1620. The original intention of the emigrants had been to land on part of the shores of Virginia ; but owing to storms, the fragile character of the vessel, and the obstinacy of the captain, they reached Cape Cod, "which is onely a headland of high hils of sand ouergrowne with shrubbie pines hurts and such trash."[2] While lying off this inhospitable promontory the emigrants with forethought bound themselves together by a social compact, thus forming a true body politic.

The Pilgrims landed at a spot "fit for habitation" in Cape Cod Harbour on the 22nd of December. Exploring expeditions were undertaken by the more adventurous under Miles Standish, a man after the type of Captain John Smith, but less boastful and of sterner religious character. No definite settlement was fixed upon and the people were therefore forced to remain in the neighbourhood of Cape Cod, where they faced the winter unprepared. Although their

---

[1] Quoted by J. R. Green, *Short History of the English People* (1893), iii. p. 1051.

[2] Smith, *A Description of New England* (1616), p. 27.

F

minister, John Robinson, had described them months before as " well-weaned from the delicate milk of the Mother country and inurred to the difficulties of a strange land," [1] yet their sufferings during those wild and stormy months must have been terrible.   Several of the party died, amongst them their first governor, William   Carver.   His   successor   was   the   already mentioned chronicler, William Bradford, who served the colony well and faithfully for twelve years.   He was the first American citizen of English birth who was selected as governor by free choice.   His strength of character, moral rectitude, and lofty public spirit made him worthy of the high office conferred upon him.   Fortunately his first year of government was freed from the burden of Indian attacks.   The truth was that the Pilgrim Fathers always preserved friendly relations with the neighbouring Redskins; partly because they had been so reduced in numbers by pestilence that they were never a serious danger, and partly owing to Edward Winslow, one of the ablest and most highly educated of the settlers, who had saved, by his knowledge of medicine, the Indian chief's life, thus establishing from the first amicable relations.

Amidst the most heart-rending adversity the Pilgrim Fathers   worked   at   the   communal   industry,   and struggled through those months of cold and semi-starvation, helped no doubt by the fact that they were religious enthusiasts filled with a sense of a divine mission.   In May 1621 Bradford records the first marriage amongst the settlers, which was conducted on somewhat novel lines, for " according to ye laudable custome of ye Low-cuntries, in which they had liued

---

[1] Quoted by J. R. Green, *op. cit.*, p. 1049.

was thought most requisite to be performed, by the magistrate."[1]   In November fifty additional settlers came out from the Leyden congregation, and these not only increased the difficulty of supplying food for everyone, but also introduced a feeling of dissatisfaction with what they found.   Bradford had, however, the laugh on his side.   On Christmas Day the Governor called them to work as usual, but "the new company . . . said it wente against their consciences to work on y^t day."   They were therefore allowed to remain at home, the rest of the colony going out to work; but when the governor came home at noon, "he found them in ye streete at play openly; some pitching ye barr & some at stoole-ball and such like sports.   So he went to them and tooke away their Implements and tould them that it was against his conscience, that they should play & others worke."[2]

The settlers had indeed laboured hard and not in vain, for a definite grant of their territory was issued by the New England Company, and there was now no fear of their log-fort, their houses, or their twenty-six acres of cleared ground being seized by the original members to whom the land had been granted by James I.   The little plot of ground thus carefully tended seems to have been a real oasis in the wilderness.   An eye-witness, Edward Winslow, has drawn an ideal picture of the settlement.   "Here are grapes, white and red, and very sweet and strong also; strawberries, gooseberries, raspas, etc.; plums of three sorts, white, black and red, being almost as good as a damson; abundance of roses, white, red and damask; single but very sweet indeed.   The country wanted

[1] Bradford, *op. cit.*, May 12.   [2] Bradford, *op. cit.*

only industrious men to employ." [1]   With such a
tempting account it is not surprising that thirty-five
new settlers went out in 1622.

The communal principle gradually began to break
down.   The younger men did not care to work so
hard and find that they gained no more than the weak
and aged ; nor were the married men pleased with the
idea of their wives cooking, washing, and sewing for
the bachelors.   As early as 1623, signs of the dis-
appearance of the system were beginning to show
themselves ; and by 1627 its break up was completed
when the interests of the London partners were
transferred to six of the chief settlers with a general
division of land and live stock.   The government of
the settlement was now placed on an assured footing ;
the laws were passed by the whole body of freemen,
who had also the double right of electing the governor
and a committee of seven assistants.   Under the new
methods the colony throve apace, and three years after
the change, two new townships were formed and these
sent delegates to an assembly which was primarily
composed of the whole body of freemen, but which,
owing to the existence of these delegates, gradually
developed, until in New Plymouth there was a
proper bicameral legislature with a governor at its
head.

The Plymouth colonists set " the example of a
compact religious brotherhood." [2]   In 1636 they
passed a code of laws which in no way clashed with
those of England, but applied more especially to the
style of life which they had adopted.   The brotherhood
extended its bounds year by year, and hardly a score

---

[1] Young, *Chronicles of the Pilgrim Fathers* (ed. 1841).
[2] Thwaites, *The Colonies*, 1492-1750 (1891), p. 123.

of years had passed since their first landing before eight prim, clean, and comfortable towns had been built, containing a population of about 3000 inhabitants. By this time the Civil War had broken out in England, but the settlers were little affected by it, for they lived their own quiet lives and went on their way, filled with religious fervour and working hard to support themselves.

After the Restoration, however, they felt bound to bestir themselves in political affairs, and in June 1661 their general court sent a petition to Charles II., asking him to confirm their liberties, explaining to him that they were his faithful subjects "who did hither transport ourselves to serve our God with a pure conscience, according to His will revealed, not a three days' journey as Moses, but near three thousand miles into a vast howling wilderness, inhabited only by barbarians." They concluded their petition in the quaintest words, saying that if only the King will grant their wishes, "we say with him, it is enough, our Joseph (or rather) our Charles is yet alive." [1]   The poverty of the Plymouth brethren about this time is evidenced by their lack of funds necessary for the renewal of their charter in 1665; and also in the fact that the people were not able to maintain scholars for their ministers, "but are necessitated to make use of a gifted brother in some places." [2]   Nevertheless in this same year they are computed to have had a fighting force of 2500 men; and on two later occasions (1676 and 1690) they were strong enough to make strenuous but ineffectual attempts to obtain a charter from the Crown.   The little colony that has perhaps the

---

[1] *Calendar of State Papers*, Colonial, 1661-1668, p. 36.
[2] *Ibid.*, p. 344.

proudest of all positions in American history was finally, in 1691, merged in its more arrogant and pushing neighbour Massachusetts, and the land of the Pilgrim Fathers lost its identity.

Just as Puritanism had been the cause of the foundation of New Plymouth, so it was in the case of Massachusetts. Lord Macaulay has pointed out that " the Puritan was made up of two different men, the one all self-abasement, penitent gratitude, passion ; the other proud, calm, inflexible, sagacious." [1]   The first type represented New Plymouth, where Puritanism was distressed, and where its followers struggled manfully but were self-abased.   Massachusetts, on the other hand, resembled the second type ; here Puritanism was vigorous ;   the upholders of the belief were aggressive, strong, determined, and pushing.   Thus the two colonies were not only different in character, but for that very reason were destined to differ in prosperity.

As early as 1620, Sir Ferdinando Gorges and others had been interested in the colonisation of New England ; and in a document issued in the following year, strict injunctions were laid down for the carrying out of material fit for the foundation of a settlement. Thus, every " shipp of three score tons shall carry wth them twoe Piggs, two Calves, twoe couple of tame Rabbetts, two couple of Hens and a cocke." [2] Nothing, however, seems to have been permanently established, and within two years this New England Company is said to have been " in a moribund condition." [3]   In 1623 some Dorchester traders started

---

[1] Macaulay, *Essays* (ed. 1891), p. 23.

[2] *American Historical Review*, vol. iv. No. 4, p. 689.

[3] *Ibid.*, p. 702.

a fishing station at Cape Ann, Massachusetts Bay.
The manager was Roger Conant, who had disagreed
with his brethren in New Plymouth and had separated
from them. Three years later the scheme was
abandoned ; most of the settlers returned except
Conant and a small band who "squatted" at Naum-
keag, better known in later years as Salem. The
failure of the merchants did not discourage John
White, incumbent of Dorchester, and he determined to
form a settlement for Puritans, from which there sprang
the colony of Massachusetts. Matters were at once
hurried on, and in 1629 six Puritan partners obtained
a grant of land from the New England Company,
which was to extend westward as far as the Pacific
Ocean, then believed to be but a short distance. One
of the partners, John Endecott, was selected to occupy
the land. On his arrival he had some trouble with
an earlier but somewhat disreputable squatter called
Morton, who had formed a little colony, Merry Mount,
where, apparently, his perfectly innocent sports, such as
dancing round the Maypole, annoyed the stern New
Englanders, and made them class such diversions as
"beastly practices." Endecott took strong measures,
and as the Maypole was particularly disgusting to the
Puritan mind, he settled the matter by hewing "down
the *infelix arbor*." [1]

A royal charter was readily granted in March 1629,
establishing the Governor and Company of Massachusetts Bay, but omitting to insist on the Company's
meetings being held in England. It was not a very
great step, therefore, to transfer the schemes of a
mere trading company to the principles of a self-
sufficing colony ; and before the end of the year the

---

[1] Doyle, *The English in America* (1887), vol. i. p. 119.

interests of the traders passed into the hands of ten persons who were particularly concerned in the prosperity of the colony, which in the future was regarded as perfectly distinct from the Company. The necessary preliminaries having been satisfactorily concluded, emigration began at once. The character of the colonists was very superior to that of the "riff-raff" that had been sent to Virginia. Some of the most intellectual clergymen of the day took a deep interest in the undertaking, a few indeed actually accompanied the three hundred and fifty settlers who embarked for their new homes.

"The first beginning of this worke seemed very dolorous," writes the chronicler, but the people were most fortunate in their choice of governor, John Winthrop. He was a man of forty-three years of age, who had received a good education at Cambridge and had some knowledge of the law; he had passed the latter years of his life, before emigration, as a Suffolk squire, and had been moulded in the school of Hampden. His character was of the best, and he is revered as one of the strongest and certainly one of the most lovable of the early settlers in America. He was a thorough Puritan, but of that type of which Charles Kingsley wrote and made so attractive. Like his brethren the governor showed humility, but unlike so many he was sweet-tempered and moderate; not that he was too gentle, for his decisive mind and sound constructive statesmanship saved him from any appearance of weakness. It may be said, in short, that Winthrop, as a man of wealth, of good birth, and of great abilities, was the most remarkable Puritan statesman in colonial history. He was assisted in his work by "the worthy Thomus Dudly, Esq.,"[1] as Deputy Governor, and Mr Simon Brodestreet as Secretary. Endecott's original settlement had been at Charlestown, where the colonists had pitched some tents of cloth and built a few small huts ; but in 1630 Winthrop moved to Boston, which became the capital, and within a few months eight small settlements were established along Boston Bay.

A regular representative assembly with governor and assistants soon became necessary, its importance being brought forward by the Watertown protest. The freemen of this settlement refused to pay a tax of £60 to fortify the new town of Cambridge, "and delivered their opinions, that it was not safe to pay moneys after that sort for fear of bringing themselves and posterity into bondage."[2] Thus it was seen that a representative assembly was indispensable ; it was not, however, until a lost pig in 1644 had caused a petty civil suit which led to a quarrel between the deputies and assistants that the Massachusetts parliament became bicameral. Long before this the colony had been regarded with disfavour in England. Archbishop Laud was only too ready to listen to any stories against the Puritans ; the colony was therefore solemnly arraigned before the Privy Council and the three chief members were questioned as to the conduct of the rest; and as an immediate consequence the intending settlers of the year 1634 were not allowed to sail without taking the oath of allegiance and promising to conform to the Book of Common Prayer. The emigrants were willing enough to subscribe to

[1] *A History of New England* (1654), p. 38.
[2] Winthrop, *The History of New England from* 1630 *to* 1649. [1633, Feb. 17.]

these as England was becoming unbearable. Laud
with his Arminian theories, Pym with his revolutionary
ideas, and Charles with his irresolution, were gradually
causing a distinct emigration to what the newcomers
imagined was a land of peace. They arrived to find
it in a bellicose state, for the fact that a royal
Commission of twelve, with Laud at the head, had
been appointed to administer the affairs of the
colonies, had so alarmed them that the colonists had
started to fortify Dorchester, Charlestown, and Castle
Island.

Nothing perhaps is more astonishing than the bitter
intolerance of those who had fled to find toleration;
but to the Puritan toleration was only significant of
indifference, and was therefore an abhorrent principle
at the very time he so sorely needed it. The religious
dissensions during the early years of the colony of
Massachusetts illustrate the fanatical and bigoted
character of the Puritan quite as clearly as any
particular event or series of events in English history.
It is painful to find even in the first few months of the
settlement, when Endecott was still in command, many
evidences of intolerance. John and Samuel Browne
collected a congregation and conducted the service
according to the Book of Common Prayer; but so
horrible did this appear to Endecott that these luck-
less men were expelled from the colony. Two years
later political and social rights were intimately
connected with religious privileges by an ordinance
that no one was to be a freeman unless he belonged
to a church; and this was still further extended
in 1635, so that no man could vote at a town meeting
unless he possessed the ecclesiastical qualification.

Religious troubles were fomented, after 1631, by

the able but bigoted Roger Williams. He was a
man of very considerable gifts, being both an energetic
and attractive preacher, but at the same time filled
with an intense hatred of Erastianism. As soon as he
arrived he was chosen minister of Salem, where he
exhibited his imperfect sense of proportion and gained
for himself the title of "a haberdasher of small
questions."[1] His energy and impulsiveness led him
astray, and the more intellectual could hardly fail to
see that his mind was incapable of distinguishing the
vital from the trifle. His political doctrines forced
him into extraordinary actions, such as that of persuading Endecott to cut the cross out of the royal
ensign ; while at the same time he not only denied
the English sovereign's right to grant territory in North
America, but also with equal vehemence repudiated all
secular control in religious affairs. For four years the
freemen of Massachusetts quietly suffered Roger
Williams' whimsicalities, but in October 1635 their
patience had come to an end, and the General Court
of the Colony banished him with twenty of his disciples,
as his sympathetic chronicler says, "and that in the
extremity of winter, forcing him to betake himselfe into
the vast wilderness to sit down amongst the Indians."[2]
The kindly governor, John Winthrop, does not seem
to have approved of the verdict, for many years afterwards Roger Williams wrote "that ever honoured
Governour Mr Winthrop privately wrote to me to steer
my course to Nahigonset Bay. . . . I took his prudent
motion as an hint and voice from God, and waving
all other thoughts and motions, I steered my course
from Salem (though in winter snow which I feel yet)

[1] Doyle, *Cambridge Modern History* (1905), vol. vii. p. 17.
[2] *Simplicities Defence against Seven-Headed Policy* (1646), p. 2.

unto these parts, wherein I may say Peniel, that is, I have seene the face of God." [1]

During the year 1635 three notable personages came to the colony. The first was Henry Vane, the younger, " who," wrote Winthrop, " being a young gentleman of excellent parts, and had been employed by his father (when he was ambassador) in foreign affairs ; yet, being called to the obedience of the gospel, forsook the honors and preferments of the court, to enjoy the ordinances of Christ in their purity here." [2] The other two recruits were, John Wheelwright, a clergyman, and his sister Mrs Anne Hutchinson, who was a woman of great learning and brilliance, but by instinct an agitator of a most indiscreet and impetuous character ; although both acute and resolute, she allowed herself to be carried away by her passion for theological controversy. Her religious views were Antinomian and were strongly opposed to the doctrines of the Puritans, who believed in justification by faith, strengthened by sanctified works. To Governor Winthrop the distinction between the two doctrines appeared to be a mere jargon of words, and he was not very far wrong when he said " no man could tell, except some few who knew the bottom of the matter, where any difference was." [3] Mrs Hutchinson soon had a large following, including Wheelwright, Thomas Hooker, and John Cotton, but the latter deserted her and refused to follow her in all her heresies. In 1636 she was strongly supported by Harry Vane, who was for a short time the governor ; but in the following year both she and her brother

[1] Massachusetts Historical Society, *Collections*, i.
[2] Winthrop, *The History of New England from* 1630 *to* 1649 (1853), vol. i. p. 170.
[3] *Ibid.*, vol i. p. 213.

were tried before the General Court and were banished as heretics.

Meantime the education of Massachusetts was not neglected, as is proved by the foundation in 1636 of Harvard College at Cambridge, for " it pleased God to stir up the heart of one Mr Harvard (a godly gentle-mad and a lover of learning, then living amongst us) to give the one halfe of his Estate (it being in all about 1700 *l.*) towards the erecting of a Colledge, and all his Library." [1]   The building was erected rapidly and was " very faire and comely within and without," [2] says an anonymous writer in 1641 ; but Charles II.'s com-missioners do not seem to have been so much impressed, as twenty years later they speak of it as a wooden college.   The great days of Harvard had not as yet arrived ; nor indeed was the learning more advanced even as late as 1680, for the whole place is described by two Dutch visitors as smelling like a tavern.   " We inquired," they say, " how many pro-fessors there were, and they replied not one, that there was no money to support one." [3]   But out of such small beginnings a great educational establishment rose which has won for itself a famous name and added lustre to the annals of the colony.

It seemed extremely likely that the war-clouds that had arisen in the Old Country might drift across the Atlantic to New England.   It was for this reason that some sort of confederation between the colonies was proposed ; and in 1643 Massachusetts, New Haven, Plymouth, and Connecticut formed the first New England Confederacy.   A distinct desire for religious and political unity had been in the air for some time,

[1] *New England's First Fruits* (1643), p. 12.   [2] *Ibid.*
[3] *Journal of a Voyage to New York in* 1679-80.

not only because of the dread of Dutch and Indian attack, but also because it was hoped that inter-colonial quarrels might be checked, and a firm and united attitude might be shown towards any encroachments on the part of the British Government.   There were, however, in this confederation two essential weaknesses which sooner or later would inevitably wreck the whole scheme.   In the first place Massachusetts was by far the largest, richest, and most prosperous of the colonies ; it was therefore called upon to contribute the largest share, but received no more than the weaker and poorer members of the Union.   Secondly, although the federal government was exactly what was wanted, it could exercise no direct control over the citizens of any particular colony.   This latter was probably the chief cause of the non-success of the confederation.   Maine and the settlements along the Narragansett Bay in vain pleaded to be enrolled in the first United States ; but they were refused as being neither sufficiently settled nor possessing political order.   The four confederate colonies bound themselves by written conditions and were denominated " The United Colonies of New England."   It was obvious from the very beginning that disagreement would come, if for no other reason because of the struggle that was taking place in England.   Massachusetts was no more for the Parliament than for the King, while the other New England colonies were as a whole sturdy supporters of Pym and his party. Disagreement bred disagreement, as is seen in the proposal to fight the Dutch in America, while Blake was winning fame in European waters.   This, however, was prevented by the commissioners of one colony standing out against the opinions of the others.   A similar lack of unity was only too apparent in 1654, when Massachusetts consented to make war against the Nyantic Indians, but the indifference and incapacity of their captain caused general dissatisfaction among the rest of the confederation.

The attitude of Massachusetts toward England during the Civil Wars was a most unsatisfactory one; it was as it were prophetic of what was to come. The contemptuous and haughty indifference shown by the colony to Cromwell was not because of any deep-seated loyalty to Charles I.; it was rather the exhibition of an independent spirit and a desire to leave England and English affairs strictly alone, if they were allowed, in turn, to live under the government of a governor and magistrates of their own choosing and under laws of their own making. This feeling does not seem to have been understood in England, and at the time of the Restoration the colony was regarded as having been Parliamentarian in its sympathies, whereas indeed it had been separatist. The Royal Commissioners in 1661 found that Massachusetts "was the last and hardest persuaded to use his Majesty's name in their forms of justice";[1] and yet in February the King was petitioned to look upon the colonists kindly and "let not the Kinge heare men's wordes: your servants are true men, fearers of God and the Kinge, not given to change, zealous of government and peaceable in Israel, we are not seditious as to the interest of Cæsar nor schismaticks as to the matters of religion."[2]

The religion of Massachusetts was, at this time, of the narrowest and most bigoted type. The colonists

[1] *Calendar of State Papers*, Colonial, 1661-1668, p. 344.
[2] *Ibid.*, p. 9.

were intolerant of any opinion save their own, and their cruel fanaticism was excited particularly against the humble and law-abiding sect of Quakers. The General Court at Boston regarded the Quakers as a positive danger to the State, and as people "who besides their absurd and blasphemous doctrines, do like rogues and vagabonds come in upon us."[1] In 1656 two Quaker women landed at Boston ; they were immediately treated with extreme brutality and finally banished to the Barbadoes. This led to further definite enactments, and at the instigation of some of the most intolerant clergy of Boston, an act was passed imposing the penalty of death in cases of extreme obstinacy. So brutal were the punishments inflicted even where no extreme obstinacy was shown that it is probable that death was preferable and welcomed by the ill-treated wretches who had fallen into the hands of these fanatics.. At the Restoration, Edward Burrough, an English Quaker, took up the case of his brethren in Massachusetts, and laid before Charles II. a list of brutalities that were only equalled by the horrors of the Inquisition. We read of men being whipped twenty-three times, receiving 370 stripes from a whip with three knotted cords ; two unhappy wretches were cut to bits by 139 blows from pitched ropes, one being "brought near unto death, much of his body being beat like unto a jelly."[2] Others were put neck and heels in irons, or burnt deeply in the hand ; some had their ears cut off by the hangman ; while many other free-born subjects of the King were "sold for bondmen and bondwomen to

---

[1] *Calendar of State Papers*, Colonial, 1661-1668, p. 32.
[2] Burrough, *A Declaration of the Sad and Great Persecution and Martyrdom of the . . . Quakers, etc.* (1660).

Barbadoes, Virginia, or any of the English Plantations."[1] Burrough succeeded in persuading the King to take some action, and the Massachusetts Council was severely reprimanded for the treatment it had meted out to the Quakers. As a result of the King's interference the General Court at Boston determined in 1661 to act with as much lenity as possible to the Quakers, but to prevent their intrusion it was recognised that "a sharp law" against them was a necessity.

During the last quarter of the seventeenth century the New England Confederacy, including Massachusetts, was disturbed by all the horrors of Indian warfare. In the year 1670 the Pokanoket Indians under their chief Metacam, or as he was generally known, King Philip, became unfriendly. For some time the warfare was not of a very serious character, but at last in 1674 an Indian convert brought news of a general attack, and paid the penalty of his fidelity to the English by being murdered by Philip or one of his braves. The Indian chief now fell upon the extreme south of New Plymouth, and fire, murder, and rapine were common throughout the land. The Puritans of Boston, under their Governor Leverett, saw in this terrible slaughter the hand of the Lord, and in November the whole city passed a day of humiliation. Within the chapels and homes their sins were openly acknowledged, but the people showed more of the spirit of the Pharisee than of the Publican in this humiliation before God. They penitently confessed that they had neglected divine service, but what was to them still worse, they had shown sinful lenity to the heretical sect of

---

[1] Burrough, *A Declaration of the Sad and Great Persecution, and Martyrdom of the . . . Quakers*, etc. (1660).

G

Quakers, and had indeed invited the Almighty's wrath by an extravagance in apparel and in wearing long hair. Pharisaical as this day of humiliation sounds, the greater number of the people were probably genuine in their attitude towards what they regarded as sin; and certainly when the time came they were ready to prove themselves sturdy fighters. It was only natural that the settlers should be successful in the end, for as a civilised people they were better armed and better organised, but their victory was delayed in the coming, and when the war was really over they found that it had cost them dear. Edward Randolph writing at the time sums up the English losses at a high figure. " The losse to the English in the severall colonies in their habitations and stock, is reckoned to amount to 150,000 l., there having been about 1200 houses burned, 8000 head of cattle great and small, killed, and many thousand bushels of wheat, pease and other grain burned . . . and upward of 3000 Indians, men, women and children destroyed." [1]   King Philip, who had caused all this destruction, was in 1676 hunted down and shot " with a brace of bullets . . . this seasonable prey was soon divided, they cut off his Head and Hands and conveyed them to Rhode Island, and quartered his Body and hung it upon four trees." [2]   With this last act of unnecessary barbarity the Indian power was broken, and Philip's war was at an end.

Meantime the administration of New England had been vested in the hands of special commissioners, whose powers were transferred to the Privy Council. Under this system, revenue officers appointed in

---

[1] Hutchinson, *A Collection of Original Papers*, etc. (1769).
[2] *The Warr in New-England Visibly Ended* (1677).

England were sent out in 1675 to enforce the Navigation Acts, which were excellent as a stimulus to English shipping, but were nevertheless retrograde with regard to the colonies. Edward Randolph was despatched to America to report upon the working of the colonial system under these famous laws, and he showed, even as early as this, that the revenue acts were openly violated by the people, who, a century later, were to be notorious for their smuggling proclivities. Massachusetts was looked upon by the home authorities with the strongest suspicion, which was still further intensified by Edward Randolph's eight specific charges against the settlers. (1) That they have no right to the land or government in any part of New England, and that they have always been regarded as usurpers ; (2) that they have formed themselves into a commonwealth, denying appeals to England, and refusing to take the oath of allegiance ; (3) that they have protected the regicides ; (4) that they coin their own money with their own impress ; (5) that in 1665 they opposed the King's commissioners with armed force ; (6) that they have put men to death for matters of religion ; (7) that they impose an oath of fidelity to their government ; (8) that they have violated all the acts of Trade and Navigation to the annual loss of £100,000 to the King's Customs. After these charges had reached England, the agents of the Massachusetts government, William Stoughton and Peter Bulkeley, were called upon to answer the serious indictment. They pleaded that they were unable to answer any other questions but those concerning the business on which they had come ; but they agreed that as private individuals they would make some kind of defence, and at the same time promised, on behalf of the settlers, amendment in the future. This submission only acted as an incentive for further attack, and Randolph now charged the "Bostoners" with denying the right of baptism to those not born in church fellowship; and also with fining certain persons for absenting themselves from the meeting-houses. The Committee of Trade and Plantations next turned to the Charter of the colony, and this was severely criticised; then the Laws of the colony were discussed, and many illegal imposts were discovered. Amongst other things it was seen that three shillings and fourpence was the fine levied for galloping in the streets of Boston; that five shillings was demanded from those who dared to observe Christmas Day, and that no less than £5 was the fine for importing playing cards; with all of which they now found serious fault, though it must be allowed that they tended to create "an ideally holy and unhappy community."[1] All this time Stoughton and Bulkeley were most anxious to return to America, but they were obliged to stay all through 1678, and it was only in 1679 that they were able to leave, because England was too busy with the Popish Plot to worry about the affairs of the far distant Massachusetts. The matter, however, was by no means finished. Randolph was determined to bring the colony to book; and when he was again sent out in 1680 to supervise the customs he at once renewed his charges. "The Bostoners, after all the protestations by their agents, are acting as high as ever, and the merchants trading as freely; no ship having been seized for irregular trading, although they did in 1677 make a second

---

[1] Fortescue, Introd. : *Calendar of State Papers*, Colonial, 1677-1680, p. xiv.

law to prevent it." [1] He then says that his life
was threatened by these smugglers, and that as
he has only life and hope left, he is unwilling to
expose himself to the rage of a bewildered
multitude. He concludes by beseeching for strong
measures, which he considers are essential, and " for
his Majesty to write more letters will signify no more
than the London Gazette." [2] This appeal had its
effect, and the King practically threatened to land
redcoats in Boston " a century before their time, when
there should be no Washington to organise resistance,
no European coalition to distract their operations, and
no French fleet and army to drive them from the
Continent." [3]

Even after this thundering declaration the actions
of the settlers were not always in accordance with
strict loyalty, and in 1684, though their agents loudly
protested, the Court of Chancery decreed the Massachusetts Charter to be null and void. James II.'s well-
intentioned efforts carried out in the wrong way by
the wrong methods, and generally by the wrong men,
deprived him of popularity both in his home dominions
and in his growing Empire in the West. His great
scheme for the colonies was one of union ; but his
action was far more destructive than anything that
George III. ever proposed or imagined. The
representative principle was snatched from the
youthful colonies ; and they were deprived of their
legislative, executive and financial rights, which were
given to a royal Governor and Council, ruling an
united province entitled New England, and bearing a
special flag of its own. The Governor appointed by

[1] *Calendar of State Papers*, Colonial, 1677-1680, p. xviii.   [2] *Ibid.*, p. 545.
[3] Fortescue, *Calendar of State Papers*, Colonial, 1677-1680, p. xxi.

the King was Colonel Sir Edmund Andros, a very active and most capable administrator, but an ardent churchman, and therefore particularly unacceptable to the Puritan colonies of the New England group.   He was by no means a young man when he arrived to take over the administration in December 1686, but with surprising energy he set about doing what he could by extending the frontier against the Indians, and establishing a line of garrisoned forts to keep them in awe.   Discontent, however, was visible on every side ; Connecticut refused to give up its charter, which, according to tradition, was hidden in an oak ; while the town of Ipswich, Mass. refused like Watertown many years earlier to pay taxes without representation.   When James issued his Declaration of Indulgence some of the best of the Massachusetts colonists imagined that it meant real toleration ; Increase Mather was one of these.   He had conducted the diplomatic relations of the colony during the struggle over the charter ; he was well-beloved as the minister of the old North Church of Boston, and as President of Harvard College.   For these reasons he was once again selected as mediator, and was deputed to plead with James on behalf of his colony, but like so many in England he found that he had come on a fruitless errand, and that genuine toleration was very far from the thoughts of the Papist King.

The news of the Revolution in England in November 1688 aroused the people of Massachusetts. Sir Edmund Andros, instead of accepting the inevitable, arrested John Winslow, the bearer of the good tidings.   The discontent which had long been simmering beneath the surface now broke out.   The

covetousness of the rulers, the ruination of trade, the
oppression of the people, and that "base drudgerie"
to which they had been put stirred them to a state
of frenzy.   Boston and Charlestown armed ; Andros
was unable to quell the fury, and he was captured by
his subordinates, who claimed that "the exercise of
Sir Edmund's commission, so contrarie to the Magna
Charta, is surely enough to call him to account by
his superiors." [1]   In this the people of New England
made a mistake, for although Andros was sent over
to England with a party of his accusers, he was only
examined by the Lords of the Committee for Trade
and Plantations, and was almost immediately released
without being finally tried.

The rule of William and Mary in England was
acknowledged willingly in Massachusetts.   A new
charter was granted to the colony, in which it was
stated that the Governor, Lieutenant-Governor and
Secretary were to be appointed by the Crown.   The
franchise was now based upon a property qualification,
and the religious oligarchy was swept away.   The
first Council was nominated by the Crown, but in
the future the members were to be selected by the
General Court.   The little colony that owed its origin
to the Pilgrim Fathers was incorporated within the
prosperous bounds of Massachusetts, which from this
date to the great schism remained a Crown colony
with distinct tendencies towards, and sometimes
clearly expressed desires of, emancipation and independence.   "It was not as though the colony
complained of grievances which could be enquired
into and put right ; it simply adopted towards

[1] Hutchinson,   *A Collection of Original Papers relative to the History
of the Colony of Massachusetts Bay* (1769).

England now openly and now by equivocation an attitude of 'hands off.'"[1]

The first Governor of the new Crown colony was that romantic character, Sir William Phipps. He was born in 1650 on a small plantation on the banks of the Kennebec; he was one of twenty-six children, and until eighteen years of age kept "sheep in the wilderness." There is little doubt that from early times he was determined to succeed, and he always prophesied that one day he would be the owner of a fair brick house in Green Lane, North Boston. According to his earliest biographer he was one of the most remarkable men of his day, being "of an Enterprising Genius and naturally disclaimed Littleness: But in his Disposition for Business was of the Dutch Mould, where with a little show of Wit, there is much Wisdom demonstrated, as can be shewn by any Nation. His Talent lay not in the Airs that serve chiefly for the pleasant and sudden Turns of Conversation; but he might say as Themistocles, Though he could not play the Fiddle, yet he knew how to make a little City become a great One. He would prudently contrive a weighty Undertaking, and then patiently pursue it unto the End. He was of an Inclination, cutting rather like a Hatchet than like a Razor."[2] Such was the character of this man, who, in 1683, found himself the Captain of a King's ship. In 1687 he was fortunate enough to discover a wrecked vessel filled with treasure, and after being entertained and knighted by James II. he returned to New England to build the "fair brick house" of which he had foretold. After the resettlement of

---

[1] Egerton, *A Short History of British Colonial Policy*, p. 62.
[2] Mather, *Magnalia Christi Americana, II.* (1702).

Massachusetts, which now practically extended from Rhode Island to New Brunswick, excluding New Hampshire, Phipps was appointed Governor. He owed his appointment to the favour of Increase Mather, but it seems to have been welcomed generally, for Phipps was at first popular, generous, and well-meaning. At the outset he was confronted by difficulties that would have baffled a man of far greater capacity. The taxation of the colony had not been specifically mentioned in the charter, and the colonists seized upon the opportunity to enact that no taxes were to be levied without the consent of the Assembly. The home government immediately rejected this, and so opened the door for the squabbles and recriminations eighty years afterwards, which led to the separation of the American colonies from the mother country. Gradually Phipps lost his popularity, which had to a certain extent been founded upon his romantic history. He became brutal, covetous and violent, and so in 1694 the Bostonians turned against him. His temper had never been calm, and it is said that by the end of his period of office he was engaged in violent quarrels with every man of importance in the province.

The governorship of the colony between 1698 and 1701 was amalgamated with those of New York, New Jersey, and New Hampshire. The Earl of Bellomont was given supreme control, and won the goodwill of the people by favouring the democratic party and recommending many reforms. His special title to Fame is his suppression of the pirates along the coasts, who according to Bellomont's complaint in 1698 had been protected and encouraged by Benjamin

Fletcher, Governor of New York. " I have likewise discovered that protections were publickly exposed to sale at the said rates to Pyrats that were of other companies . . . and made discovery of the bonds the Pyrates entered into to Coll : Fletcher when he granted them Commissions." [1]   Bellomont was determined to save the colonies from these sea-wolves, and in 1701 he had the satisfaction, just before he died, of bringing the infamous Captain Kidd to the gallows.

The later history of Massachusetts must be left to the chapter on French Aggression. The colony founded first as a trading Company by a few adventurous Puritans had in seventy years become not only one of the most prosperous, but also one of the largest of the thirteen States. It had embraced several of the smaller and weaker settlements, the history of one of which has already been traced ; the story of the others has yet to be told.

[1] O'Callaghan, editor, *Documents relative to the Colonial History of the State of New York* (1854).

CHAPTER V

CONNECTICUT ; RHODE ISLAND AND PROVIDENCE
PLANTATION ; NEW HAVEN ; MAINE ; NEW HAMP-
SHIRE

THE early history of the group of colonies which
is now to engage the attention is less interesting than that of either Virginia or Massachusetts.
There is not the glamour of a first colony as in the
case of Virginia ; the men were not Pilgrim Fathers
in the true sense as in Plymouth ; the prosperity of
Massachusetts, the rivalries of Maryland, and the
Spanish danger in the Carolinas, are all wanting in
this portion of New England. There is therefore not
only a lack of romance, but there is too a pettiness
in the quarrels which continually occurred in these
colonies.

The New England Company, when once it had
started an active existence, made every effort to extract
some advantage from the land which had been
granted to it. In 1631 Lord Saye and Sele, Lord
Brooke and others obtained from the Company a
tract of land in the rich valley of the Connecticut
River. Very little, however, came of this scheme ;
and the first true settlement was made against the
strenuous opposition of the Dutch, by a party from
New Plymouth. A fresh influx of settlers came from
the already rising colony of Massachusetts, for they

had found that the land was somewhat sterile, at any rate not sufficiently fertile to support them all. The settlers on the Connecticut came from the town of Dorchester, and planted themselves at Windsor, to the disgust of the New Plymouth settlers, who were at last forced to retire. This proved, as often enough in future years, that the unscrupulous and over-bearing temper of the men of Massachusetts earned for them a reward which they did not deserve. The patentees, seeing their rights invaded by these Dorchester fili-busters, sent out a small party to establish their privileges, but these in turn were routed, and the men of Massachusetts were left in possession, though contrary to the wishes of their mother-settlement. When, however, the versatile John Winthrop, son of the more statesmanlike Governor, arrived with a com-mission as Governor of the new colony on behalf of the patentees, Massachusetts ceased to complain, and allowed the secession to become complete. Within two years the new colony of Connecticut had a population of eight hundred men, women and children, grouped in three towns, Hartford, Wethers-field, and Windsor. The freemen of these towns declared in 1638 that their constitution was the same as that of Massachusetts; but there was one great dissimilarity, for no religious test was imposed. This constitution occupies a famous place in the world's history, for not only was it the first written constitu-tion that actually created a government, but it has also been characterised as " the oldest political con-stitution in America." [1] By means of this important document, issued in January 1639, all possible claims to sovereignty on the part of Massachusetts were

[1] Bryce, *American Commonwealth.*

placed on one side for ever ; or was there any reference to the sovereignty of Charles I. or the home parliament. The document was merely an agreement amongst the colonists themselves, and by abstaining from any religious tests, or intolerance, they earned the gratitude and admiration of mankind, and throughout the whole colonial period bravely sustained this liberal spirit which had distinguished them so early in their history.

Before accomplishing this great work the colonists had a hard fight for existence against the Pequod Indians. As early as 1633 a Virginian ship's captain, Stone, was killed by this tribe near the mouth of the Connecticut River ; two years later John Oldham, a trader, was also murdered by a party of Narragansetts inhabiting Block Island. It was evident that the redskins must be taught a severe lesson if Englishmen were to live in peace. Endecott, with a small force from Massachusetts, was despatched to punish the Narragansetts, but he utterly failed in his attack upon the island tribe. In retaliation the settlers in Connecticut were surrounded by the murderous Pequods, and cut off from the sea ; fortunately, Roger Williams, having the confidence and goodwill of the redskins, managed, at this time of trial, to obtain the neutrality of the Narragansetts. This was a great advantage, as Massachusetts deserted the new settlement, leaving it to fight its own battles. Leaders with plenty of courage were not wanting, and Captains Mason and Underhill, with ninety men, marched against the Pequods. Two hundred of these tribesmen had attacked Wethersfield, and "having put poles in their Conoos, as we put Masts in our boats, and upon them hung our English mens and womens shirts and smocks in stead of sayles, and in way of bravado came along in sight of us as we stood upon Seybrooke Fort." [1] Captain John Mason was not the man to be discouraged by such war-like displays, and with considerable strategy attacked them on the flank and assaulted their chief stronghold.   The action was a hot one, for although only two Englishmen were slain, many were wounded, and six hundred Pequods are reported to have fallen.   The men of Connecticut were desperate, and fighting for their lives.   They were determined to annihilate the Pequod tribe once for all, and to establish peace by means of a sanguinary slaughter. Their actions may appear brutal, but they were necessary as Captain John Underhill took care to explain.   "Great and dolefull was the bloudy sight to the view of young souldiers that never had beene in Warre, to see so many soules lie gasping on the ground so thicke in some places, that you could hardly passe along.   It may be demanded, Why should you be so furious (as some have said), should not christians have more mercy and compassion?   But I would refer you to David's warre, when a people is growne to such a height of bloud and sinne against God and man, and all confederates in the action, there hee hath no respect to persons, but harrowes them and sawes them and puts them to the sword." [2]   This massacre and total destruction of the Pequods had the important effect of reversing the territorial relations between the English and the Indians ; direct communication between the mouth of the Connecticut and Boston was now made possible, and some form of union could only be a matter of time.

[1] Underhill, *Newes from America* (1638).   [2] *Ibid.*

As has already been shown Connecticut did join in such an union when it entered into the Confederation of New England in 1643, and it was as a member of that group that it passed through the period of the civil wars. With the Restoration the ambitions of the settlers increased, and in 1661 John Winthrop went to England to obtain a charter which would define the boundaries of the colony, and include within it the smaller settlement of New Haven, the members of which protested in vain. The patent of incorporation was granted in 1662, and the document concludes with the words which illustrate the interesting but absurd legal fiction under which the King granted land in America. The Governor and Company of the English colonists of Connecticut are to hold "the same of his Majesty, his heirs and successors as of the manor of East Greenwich in free and common soccage, yielding the fifth part of all gold or silver ore." [1] So ridiculous was this fiction that the colonists were actually supposed to be represented in the home parliament by the member of the borough containing the manor of East Greenwich. It is not surprising that even as early as this period these rigid Presbyterians felt that if the actions of the home government endangered their welfare they would be justified in ignoring that authority, and relying only upon the common weal as supreme law in the colony. But though they regarded with jealousy any attempt to limit their rights, they were too weak, owing to internal dissension, to throw off the yoke of the home authorities. They had in no way added to their strength by the incorporation of New Haven, but rather increased their weakness. This unstable con-

---

[1] *Calendar of State Papers*, Colonial, 1661-1668, p. 88.

dition is illustrated in particular, first by the emigration of the people of the town of Branford, who, armed with their civil and ecclesiastical records, preferred to occupy lands near the Delaware rather than stay under the jurisdiction of Connecticut; and secondly by the description of Connecticut itself, as recorded by the Governor, William Leete, in 1680. He shows that for the last seven years the popularity of the colony had evidently declined in England, for only one or two settlers had come from the home country each year. The population had certainly increased by about five hundred in eight years; from 2050 in 1671 to 2507 in 1679; but there was very little unity of feeling or purpose owing to the religious sects being peculiarly mixed, some being Presbyterians, some "strict congregational men," some "more large congregational men," some Quakers, and four or five are classified by the Governor as "seven-day men." [1]

For twenty-three years the people of Connecticut imagined that they enjoyed the benefits of the charter gained by Winthrop in 1662, "ye advantages and priviledges whereof made us indeed a very happy people; and by ye blessing of God upon our endeavours we have made a considerable improvement of your dominions here, which with ye defense of ourselves from ye force of both forraign and intestine enemies has cost us much expence of treasure & blood." [2]   James II., however, cared for none of these things; the charter was forfeited in 1685; and like Massachusetts, Connecticut felt the heavy hand of the too zealous Sir Edmund Andros. Being

[1] *Calendar of State Papers*, Colonial, 1677-1680, p. 577.
[2] *Ibid.*

"commissionated by his Majesty,"[1] Andros appeared with sixty grenadiers in 1687 at Hartford, and took over the government. On his capture, as already recorded, the people of Connecticut in May 1689 joyfully fell back upon their old form of government under the late charter, the forfeiture of which had been declared illegal in England.

Owing to King William's War, Connecticut was within an ace of losing its government, and for purposes of defence being united, in 1690, with its stronger neighbour New York; the proposals fell through, and the fears of the citizens were set at rest by a legal confirmation of their constitution. The colony from this time undoubtedly advanced. Its system of government was active and vigorous; each township controlled its own affairs, and in the early years of the eighteenth century local government lay entirely in the hands of the Select-men, to the exclusion of English officials. At the same time education was encouraged; a college was established by the clergy in 1698, which found its final home at Newhaven in 1717. Before this printing had been undertaken, the first press being erected in 1709 at New London; the immediate work done was not of a first-rate character, but it was the beginning of better things. At the same time it is only fair to point out that the colony was cursed by the presence of turbulent and quarrelsome negro and mulatto slaves; it was regarded with suspicion by the English governors as a protector of pirates; and it certainly must be blamed for its niggardly contributions of both men and money in the great expeditions against the French.

[1] *Calendar of State Papers*, Colonial, 1685-1688, p. 472.

H

Connecticut was not the only settlement that was partly formed by a secession from the parent colony of Massachusetts ; nor was it an isolated example of colonial establishments, for during the same period several other colonies grew up along the Eastern sea-board.   The Reverend Roger Williams, after his banishment from Massachusetts in October 1635, purchased land from the Indians, and with twelve other householders settled at Providence, by the advice of Mr Winslow, the Governor of New Plymouth. Thus Williams was able to describe himself many years later as "by God's mercy the first beginner of the mother town of Providence and of the Colony of Rhode Island." [1]   Williams' settlers immediately started a simple form of government, by which all freemen were to hold quarterly meetings and settle judicial questions, while five Select men were to transact all executive business.   Following Williams' example, Mrs Anne Hutchinson, as another refugee from the intolerance of Massachusetts, came to much the same district in 1637.   She purchased from the Indians the island of Aquedneck, or, as it was afterwards known, Rhode Island.   Her heretical followers soon founded the town of Portsmouth, and here the government was carried on by William Coddington as judge.   Mrs Hutchinson, having now time for inventing new heresies, almost immediately caused a fresh secession, and some of her hitherto ardent admirers, finding her new doctrines intolerable, left Portsmouth, and under Coddington established themselves at Newport. The colonies were reunited in 1640, with Coddington as Governor, and a regular government was

---

[1] *Calendar of State Papers*, Colonial, 1677-1680, p. 398.

instituted composed of two "assistants" from each township.

Providence and Rhode Island were regarded with dislike and suspicion by all the other colonies, being classified as the asylum for sectaries, the hot-bed of anarchy, and the true home of extreme democracy. This attitude is not surprising when it is remembered that both colonies owed their existence to parties of religious outcasts. Rhode Island nevertheless prospered, although throughout the first few years of its existence it was the centre of disorder, bickerings, and factious quarrels. At the bottom of most of the trouble was Samuel Gorton, a contentious and troublesome man, leader of a band of fanatics, who had forced themselves upon a party of Williams' settlers at Pawtuxet. The settlers appealed to Massachusetts to remove him as "a proud and pestilent seducer";[1] and had indeed placed themselves under the jurisdiction of that colony for this very purpose. In 1643, Gorton, of "insolent and riotous carriage," with nine of his followers, was imprisoned for some months at Boston, for blasphemy. The quarrel, however, did not end here. It was carried by Gorton to England, where he appealed to the Parliamentary Commissioners, who commanded the General Court to allow Gorton and his band to dwell in peace. This, at last, the Massachusetts' government consented to do with contemptuous indifference, but when Gorton pleaded for their protection against the Indians he pleaded in vain.

In the same year as the conclusion of the Gorton controversy, Providence, Portsmouth and Newport, combined into a properly constituted community.

---

[1] Quoted by Doyle, *Puritan Colonies* (1887), vol. i. p. 249.

This was the outcome of a visit paid to England in 1643 by Roger Williams, who asked for a definite charter of incorporation. In 1647, therefore, a general assembly of freemen, governor and assistants, with a court of commissioners, was established for the "Colony of Rhode Island and Providence Plantation." At first the assembly met in the different towns by rotation, and the method of voting was most complicated and non-progressive; every matter had to be voted on in each town, and was to be considered as lost unless it was carried by a majority in every town. So complex a system proved inadequate, and in 1664 an ordinary representative assembly was created. What was equally important and showed Rhode Island to be more enlightened than most of the other colonies, was the clear announcement of the doctrine of freedom of conscience to all who "live civilly." To the annoyance of Massachusetts the Rhode Island authorities consistently adhered to this doctrine, and refused to join in the barbarous persecutions of the Quakers.

The settlers expressly thanked Charles II. for sending Commissioners, and made great demonstration of their loyalty and obedience in 1665. Such actions are rather surprising in a Puritan colony, but they may have been due to the King's grant of a charter, two years before, in which they obtained a definition of their boundaries. The colony of this period was described with some minuteness by the Commissioners, who called attention to the fact that Quakers and Generalists were admitted, and that owing to the variety of sects there were no places for the worship of God, "but they sometimes associate in one house,

and sometimes in another."[1]   The colony certainly did
not advance with the strides that had been made by
Massachusetts, and the people were still extremely
unpopular with the other colonists, being denounced
on one occasion as " scum and dregs."   Nevertheless
under the government of Peleg Sandford in 1680,
Rhode Island was a small, happy, self-sufficing colony.
The chief town was Newport, built almost entirely of
timber.   As to exterior commerce it seems to have
been non-existent ; "wee have no shippinge belong-
inge to our Colloney, but only a few sloopes," and " as
for Merchants wee have none, but the most of our
Colloney live comfortably by improvinge the wilder-
nesse."[2]

This happy state of affairs was somewhat rudely
disturbed by James II.'s action in depriving Rhode
Island and Providence Plantation of that charter of
which they were so proud, and which gave " full liberty
of conscience provided that the pretence of liberty
extend not to licentiousnesse."[3] James' harsh treatment
did not last for long, and to the joy of the inhabitants
after the Revolution the action of the Papist King was
declared illegal.   A time of peace and prosperity now
followed.   From 1696 to 1726 Rhode Island increased in wealth and population, under the annually
elected Governor, Samuel Cranston, who, during these
thirty years of office, proved himself a firm, popular,
and successful administrator.

During the year in which Rhode Island was
established, another colony, New Haven, was founded
to the South.   In 1637 Theophilus Eaton, a leader in

[1] *Calendar of State Papers*, Colonial, 1661-1668, p. 343.
[2] Arnold, *History of the State of Rhode Island and Providence Plantations* (1859).
[3] *Ibid.*

the Baltic Company, and " of great esteem for religion," [1]
together with a party of settlers who were wealthier
men than most colonists, settled at the mouth of the
Quinipiac River, facing Long Island. The religious
beliefs of the settlers were of the most bigoted kind ;
their freemen were strictly limited to Church members ;
and their minister, " the reverend, judicious and godly
Mr John Davenport," [2] asserted that the scripture
was sufficient guide for all civil affairs. They soon
found " a fit place to erect a Toune, which they built
in very little time, and with very faire houses and
compleat streets ; but in a little time they over-
stockt it with Chattell, although many of them did
follow merchandizing and Maritime affairs, but their
remoteness from Mattachusets Bay, where the chiefe
traffique lay, hindered them much." [3]   Ten years
after its foundation, the colony was seen to be commercially on the decline, although other towns had grown
up such as Guildford, Milford, and Stamford. They were
all governed as one town without representation, and
the executive was placed in the hands of an elected
Governor and four assistants. The commercial depres-
sion did not last for long ; trade began to increase
again, and Newhaven became a flourishing state, the
inhabitants of which were noted for the magnificence
of their buildings and their astonishing opulence.

After the Restoration the colony fell under the
displeasure of the Crown. Two of the regicides,
William Goffe and Edward Whalley had, first, come
to Boston, then to Connecticut, and finally to New
Haven. The home government ordered their arrest,

---

[1] Winthrop, *History of New England* (1853), vol. i. p. 226.
[2] Johnson, *A History of New England*, etc. (1654.
[3] *Ibid.*

and Winthrop was very active in sending these orders
to the Governors of the different colonies, including the
Governor of New Haven, who knew that these men
had come within his rights of jurisdiction but took no
steps to effect there arrest.   For some time the King
had had strong doubts as to the loyalty of New
England as a whole ; here, in any case, was a colony
that needed watching ; and so, in 1662, as has already been shown, New Haven was absorbed by
Connecticut.   There can be no doubt that Charles
had now struck two hearty blows against the much
vaunted New England Confederation.   His refusal to
allow the ill-treatment of the Quakers, and his punishment of New Haven, were sufficient to make the
Confederation nothing more important than a triennial
meeting of federal commissioners, who sat till 1684,
but whose powers were nil, whose mutual beliefs were
non-existent, and who were only in complete concord
in resistance to the Indian raids.

Maine was yet another colony of New England,
which had a purely independent foundation, but which
was destined to be absorbed by its more prosperous
neighbour.   As early as 1623, Levitt established a
settlement on Casco Bay ;[1] while at the same time,
Sir Ferdinando Gorges, "the Father of English Colonisation in North America," [2] made a plantation at Saco.
He followed this up by the formation of a company
in 1631, but four years later the whole territory then
called New Somersetshire was granted to Gorges.
Five years later he received from Charles I. a charter
granting to him " all that part and portion of New
England lying and between the River Pascataway . . .

[1] *Mass. Hist. Col.*, Series iii., vol. viii. p. 171.
[2] *American Historical Review*, vol. iv, No. 4, p. 683.

to Kenebeck even as far as the head thereof."[1]   Sir Ferdinando very soon drew up a most grotesque constitution for his colony, creating almost more officials than there were citizens, and whose titles were very magnificent, but quite meaningless.   In exactly the same district the New England Company claimed to have proprietary rights, and it was not long before many semi-independent settlements were made in the neighbourhood of Gorges Colony.

The Civil War having broken out in 1642 Sir Ferdinando Gorges was too much engaged at home to pay any attention to Maine, " for when he was between three and four score years of age did personally engage in our Royal Martyr's service ; and particularly in the siege of Bristow, and was plundered and imprisoned several times, by reason whereof he was discountenanced by the pretended Commissioners for foreign plantations."[2]   Soon after his exploits at Bristol, Gorges died after proving himself a man of resolute purpose, but endowed with narrow ideas.   He had certainly taken an active part in the struggle for gain and position amongst a large number of the most worthless and servile courtiers, but still around him and his memory there is a halo of grandeur, borrowed perhaps from the generation to which he really belonged, nevertheless reflecting upon his person something of that glory that ought to belong to him who was the last figure of that grand procession of giants which numbered amongst its train, Gilbert and Drake, Smith and Raleigh.

No sooner had Gorges passed away than Edward Rigby claimed the whole of Maine under a grant from

[1] Josselyn, *An Account of Two Voyages to New England* (1675).
[2] *Ibid.*

the New England Company.   Against this the heirs
of Sir Ferdinando put in a strong counter-claim ; the
decision between the disputants was left to the
authorities in Massachusetts, who divided the towns
into equal halves, three being allotted to Rigby, and
three to the Gorges claimant.   The inhabitants of the
colony were not consulted, and in 1649 they took the
matter into their own hands and declared themselves
a body politic with an elective governor and council.
But this was not to last.   In the early days of the
settlement the colonists showed no signs of religious
bigotry or of any religious views at all, but gradually
they came to sympathise with both the religion and
the political opinions of Massachusetts, so that between
1651 and 1658 the townships of Maine readily accepted the authority of the greater colony.

Soon after the Restoration, Ferdinando Gorges, the
grandson of the original patentee, sought to assert his
authority over Maine, but his exertions were not
supported by the Crown, and he was unsuccessful.
In 1665 the home authorities set up a provisional
government in the colony, but concerning its history
very little is known.   According to the Commissioners
of that year the inhabitants themselves petitioned that
they might continue under his Majesty's immediate
government.   They expressed their gratitude to
Charles II. for his "fatherly care of them after
so long a death inflicted on their minds and
fortunes by the usurpation of the Massachusetts
power,"[1] and they ask that the insults of others
towards them may be prevented for the future by
the appointment of Sir Robert Carr as their
governor.   But this statement seems very improb-

[1] *Calendar of State Papers*, Colonial, 1661-1668, p. 315.

able and can hardly have expressed the general wishes of the people.

It is not surprising that Sir Robert Carr was anxious to obtain the government of the colony, as from contemporary descriptions it appears to have been a fertile and productive territory. " In these Provinces are great store of wild ducks, geese, and deer, strawberries, raspberries, gooseberries, barberries, bilberries, several sorts of oaks and pines, chestnuts and walnuts, sometimes four or five miles together ; the more northerly the country, the better the timber is accounted." [1]   The true value of Maine was realised by William Dyre, who pointed out to Charles II. the manifold advantages that he would gain if he purchased Maine for himself. By such an action the King would have absolute dominion over those seas and might settle a duty on all fisheries there ; at the same time he might very easily reduce the turbulent spirits in Massachusetts "to a ready subjection," while enriching himself with masts, tar, timber, etc., and thus " conduce to the safety of his maritime affairs." [2]   There were, however, other very different views on Maine, and John Josselyn, an Englishmen of good family, does not speak well of either the country or its inhabitants, but there are reasons for supposing that he may have been maliciously inclined. The people of Maine in 1675 "may be divided," he writes, " into Magistrates, Husbandmen or Planters, and fishermen ; of the magistrates some be Royalists, the rest perverse Spirits, the like are the planters and fishers. . . . The planters are or should be restless pains takers, providing for their Cattle, planting and sowing of Corn . . . but if they be of

[1] *Calendar of State Papers*, Colonial, 1661-1668, p. 348.
[2] *Ibid.*, 1669-1674, p. 579.

a droanish disposition as some are, they become wretchedly poor and miserable. . . . They have a custom of taking Tobacco, sleeping at noon, sitting long at meals sometimes four times in a day, and now and then drinking a dram of the bottle extraordinarily." [1]

The people of Maine may have been all that Josselyn said, but it is far from likely. They were sufficiently alert to resent the government of the Crown, and in 1668 the majority of the settlers acquiesced in the reassertion of authority by Massachusetts. For ten years the quarrel between Ferdinando Gorges and Massachusetts continued, but in 1678, although his grandfather is reported to have spent £20,000 on the colony, the grandson's claims were extinguished by the purchase of his rights for £1250. From this moment Maine ceased to exist as a separate colony, and continued incorporated with Massachusetts for many years.

The last of this early group of colonies was New Hampshire, which, in turn, like its weaker brethren, became amalgamated with the colony of Massachusetts. Early in the reign of Charles I., Captain John Mason, with Sir Ferdinando Gorges and others, formed for colonial purposes the Laconia Company. When Gorges was granted rights in Maine in 1635, Captain John Mason also received a grant of territory to the south, where a settlement was formed, and though by no means a true political community, was called New Hampshire. Mason died soon after the naming of his colony and received no benefits from his grant, which had embraced two earlier settlements : the first founded by David Thompson near the Piscataqua ; the second

---

[1] Josselyn, *ut supra.*

fifteen miles up the Cocheco, founded by Bristol and Shrewsbury merchants, who had transferred their rights to Lord Saye and Sele and Lord Brooke. It was in this latter stretch of territory that purely independent settlements were made, such as Dover, Exeter, and Hampton. The latter town, realising its weakness as an independent community, soon chose to be regarded as within the jurisdiction of Massachusetts.

The authorities of Massachusetts undoubtedly suffered from "earth hunger," and the transfer of Hampton was merely the first of a series of aggressions, for between 1642 and 1643 the other towns of New Hampshire were swallowed within the greedy maw of the stronger colony. No remonstrance came from England, for the people of the home country had enough difficulties to contend with ; while the Mason family appear to have made no serious attempts to recover their rights. After the Restoration, however, following the example of Ferdinando Gorges, the heirs of Mason petitioned the Privy Council to restore to them the rights and privileges contained in the grant of 1635. The law officers of the Crown took the matter into serious consideration, and although their verdict was against the Mason family, they declared at the same time that the colony of New Hampshire was outside the jurisdiction of Massachusetts, which had annexed it and wrongfully renamed it Norfolk. This was one more blow for the New England Confederation and for Massachusetts in particular. The King and his ministers were only too pleased to have had such an opportunity, for the Royal Commissioners had but recently accused Massachusetts of disloyalty. They had, in fact, declared that unless the King

punished the authorities, the well-affected inhabitants
would never dare to own themselves loyal subjects.
To better effect the total subjugation of the colony,
one of the Commissioners, Sir Robert Carr, proposed
that he should be made governor of New Hampshire,
a proposal which shows only too clearly the selfish
aims of the Crown officials. The actual state of New
Hampshire did not seem to trouble the Commissioners,
and whilst the bickering between the home country
and Massachusetts continued, the unfortunate inhabitants of New Hampshire were suffering all the
horrors of the already mentioned King Philip's Indian
war. For this reason the settlers took the matter
into their own hands and turned to the more powerful
colony of Massachusetts for assistance and protection.
In 1678 the inhabitants of Portsmouth and Dover
supplicated the Crown to be kept under the jurisdiction of the stronger colony. The petition from Dover
is particularly noteworthy because of its tawdry character. The petitioners speak of the favour of his
Majesty, " which like the sweet influences of superior
or heavenly bodies to the tender plants have cherished
us in our weaker beginnings, having been continued
through your special grace, under your Majesty's
protection and government of the Massachusetts, to
which we voluntarily subjected ourselves many
years ago, yet not without some necessity in part
felt for want of government and in part feared
upon the account of protection." [1] In spite of this
petition the Crown created New Hampshire a
separate province, with a council and representative
assembly. The first governor selected was John
Cutts, " a very just and honest but ancient and

[1] *Calendar of State Papers*, 1677-1680, p. 211.

infirm man,"[1] and with his appointment the people of Massachusetts revoked all former commissions.

The colony did not forget its old guardian, and looked upon it always with loyal affection, a feeling which was intensified during the tyrannical governorship of Edward Cranfield. From 1682 to 1685 this man's disgraceful conduct was tolerated, but at last the men of New Hampshire could bear his despotism no longer, broke into open rebellion, and Cranfield fled for refuge to the West Indies. The desired result was immediately obtained, for New Hampshire was reunited to Massachusetts. This, however, was not to last for long, for after the Revolution in England the proprietorship of New Hampshire was again debated. Samuel Allen had purchased from the heirs of Captain Mason any rights which they continued to imagine they possessed ; and by the corrupt connivance of an English official, Allen succeeded in obtaining a proprietary governorship with a council partly nominated by the Crown and partly by himself. It is a remarkable fact that, unlike the other colonies at this time, New Hampshire obtained no charter. The only freedom allowed to its inhabitants was the exercise of a few independent rights by means of the representative assembly elected by the freeholders.

The acceptance of the Revolution in America marks an epoch of American history. All the New England colonies had been established, and had either proved themselves sturdy enough to stand alone, or had been forced to find shelter beneath the wing of the more powerful Connecticut or Massachusetts. The New England Confederation had been tried and

[1] *Calendar of State Papers*, 1677-1680, p. 488.

found wanting. The time for union was evidently
not ripe, but this embryo of the United States ceased
to exist at identically the hour it was most wanted.
A union of all the colonies was what might have been
expected when French aggression and Canadian pluck
taxed all the resources of the colonists ; the scheme of
union, however, failed, and the French had to be met
in that haphazard and unprepared way in which, it
would appear from history, Englishmen are accustomed
not only to meet supreme danger, but to come through
it with success.

CHAPTER VI

THE FIGHT WITH THE DUTCH FOR THEIR SETTLEMENT OF NEW NETHERLAND

A NEW epoch in colonial history was reached when England adopted a warlike policy to obtain mastery in the West. During the Protectorate, England and Holland were for the first time engaged in desperate warfare. The numerous common interests that existed in the two countries, such as religion and republicanism, were of no avail to keep the peace. The war that brought such honour to Admiral Blake was not a war against a " natural enemy," but rather a contest between trade rivals using the same methods and having the same opinions. The spirit which animated Cromwell in naval affairs was not Puritanic ; it was rather that of the Elizabethan epoch. The old naval enthusiasm which had so long slept in the stagnant days of the first Stuarts had now awakened with renewed vigour, as if its long years of drowsiness had afforded true refreshment. The celebrated Navigation Act, " the legislative monument of the Commonwealth,"[1] was the outward and visible sign of this change in 1651. " It was the first manifestation of the newly awakened consciousness of the community, the act which laid the foundation of the English commercial empire. . . . It consummated the work which

[1] Seeley, *Growth of British Policy* (1897), vol. ii. p. 25.

had been commenced by Drake, discussed and ex-
pounded by Raleigh, continued by Roe, Smith,
Winthrop, and Calvert."[1] The Dutch, "the
Phœnicians of the modern world, the waggoners of
all seas,"[2] were severely injured by the new law, for
goods were no longer to be imported into England
save in English vessels or those vessels belonging to
the country of which the goods were the natural
product or manufacture. This important protective
enactment was reissued in the reign of Charles
II., and, as on the former occasion, it was one
of the main causes of embroiling England and
Holland.

For the proper enforcement of the Navigation Act,
the English colonies in the West required a geographical
compactness which in the central period of the seventeenth century they did not possess. A formidable
foreign rival held a valuable commercial settlement
between the northern and southern colonies, for the
Dutch possessed in New Amsterdam the very best
harbour along the coast. By the reign of Charles II.
the hatred of the Dutch had become a passion amongst
Englishmen, and it had not only been fostered by the
Cromwellian war, but by trade-jealousy both in the
East and in the West. In America the rising colonies
of New England, in particular, looked with greedy
eyes upon the splendid water-way of the River Hudson,
which was the finest route for Indian trade. They
had, too, suffered at the hands of their rivals; both
the settlements in Connecticut and Long Island had
for many years engaged in innumerable land disputes with the Dutch, nor did the people of New

---

[1] Seeley, *Growth of British Policy* (1897), vol. ii. p. 25.
[2] Quoted by Fitchett, *Fights for the Flag* (1900), p. 3.

I

Haven forget that some of their brethren had been
driven out of New Sweden, which the Dutch now
held.

The Dutch had made their first settlement in 1626
as an outcome of the foundation of the Dutch West
India Company five years before.   In its functions
this corporation very closely resembled the English
East India Company, for it made a special combination
of naval and commercial affairs, and almost its first
work was the establishment of the New Netherland
settlement on Long Island and along the River
Hudson.   Their chief town was planted on Man-
hattan Island and called New Amsterdam, the population of which soon after its foundation was 270 souls.
A contemporary narrative speaks cheerfully of the
probable success of the colony, and states that they
had a prosperous beginning and that " the natives of
New Netherland are very well disposed so long as
no injury is done them." [1]   But from the very first
the governors were bad ; it was in fact irregularities
in administration and want of enterprise and courage
that caused the recall of Van Twiller in 1637.   His
successor Kieft proved himself equally incapable, for
he was arbitrary and ill-advised, earning the detesta-
tion of both Dutch patroons and English settlers.
The colonists themselves were few and poor, and the
methods employed by the Company lacked any trace
of liberality or real knowledge of colonial affairs.
Peter Stuyvesant, " that resolute soldier," came into
office in 1647 ; he was the best governor who up to
that time had been sent out, but he was nothing more
than a martinet, without either sympathy or flexi-
bility.   Van der Douch in 1650 described the colony

[1] *Description and First Settlement of New Netherland* (1888).

as sadly decayed, and gave as the reasons that " the Managers of the Company adopted a wrong course at first, and as we think had more regard for their own interests than for the welfare of the country. . . . It seems as if from the first the Company have sought to stock this land with their own *employés*, which was a great mistake, for when their time was out, they returned home. . . . Trade, without which, when it is legitimate, no country is prosperous, is by their acts so decayed that the like is nowhere else. It is more suited for slaves than freemen in consequence of the restrictions upon it . . . we would speak well of the government . . . under Director Stuyvesant, which still stands, if indeed that may be called standing, which lies completely under foot." [1]

It may have been this complaint or feelings similar to those stated therein that forced Stuyvesant to do something that would show that his rule over the colony had a stimulating effect. He had regarded for some time with jealousy the little settlement of New Sweden, or as it was known in later years, Delaware. This colony had been established by one Minuit, who had been formerly employed by the Dutch West India Company. He was a friend of William Usselinx or Ussling, who had as early as 1624 obtained a charter from Gustavus Adolphus for a trading company " to Asia, Africa, America, and Magellanica." [2] But it was not until 1638 that Minuit's Swedish following arrived in America and erected Fort Christina, named after that extraordinary royal tomboy, the Queen of Sweden. They soon

[1] *The Representation of New Netherland* (ed. 1849).
[2] *Documents relative to the Colonial History of the State of New York* (1877).

had so far settled themselves as to be strong enough to drive out a party from New Haven, but they had not calculated on the hostility of the Dutch.   Stuyvesant was determined to seize New Sweden, and set out in 1651 to exert Dutch rights, and for their protection established Fort Casimir on the site of what is now Newcastle, Del.   This was merely the beginning of a larger policy of annexation, which was accomplished in 1655 when the Swedish settlement passed into the hands of the Dutch without bloodshed on the appearance of the Governor with an army of 700 men.   The conquered territory was immediately sold to the city of Amsterdam and a colony was established there under the name of New Amstel.   On the surface this energetic policy had much to recommend it from the Dutch point of view ; but in reality the people of the New Netherlands gained but little, as in that colony there were no popular institutions, no true self-government, and not even the advantage of a really efficient despotism to give interior strength or possibilities of exterior advance.   The fact was that Stuyvesant's action resulted only in harm to his colony, for in carrying out the extirpation of the Swedish settlement in Delaware he absolutely drained his own resources and left himself unprepared and incapable of resisting the onslaught of the English.

The crushing blow fell in August 1664.   In the March of that year Charles II. granted to his brother James, Duke of York, all the territory then held by the Dutch, on the plea that it was really British soil by right of discovery.   This was the mere reassertion of an old claim, for James I. had demanded the territory by right of " occupancy " as early as 1621, and Charles I.

did the same by "first discovery, occupation, and possession"; Cromwell too had attempted to make possession a real thing in 1654, but the first Dutch War ended too soon. The action of Charles II. may well be regarded as a very practical declaration of war. Colonel Richard Nicolls was appointed to seize the New Netherlands. He was the most important of the Commissioners sent out to report on the state of the colonies, and was a good soldier, a man of great courage, but at the same time forbearing and lenient. The colony which he was ordered to attack contained a population of about 1500 souls, 600 of whom were of English stock, dwelling for the most part on Long Island, which was partially Anglicised by an influx of settlers from Connecticut and New Haven. At the end of August Nicolls arrived off New Amsterdam with four ships, and 450 soldiers and Connecticut volunteers. On September 4 he sent terms to Stuyvesant, stating that "His Majesty, being tender of the effusion of Christian blood, confirms and secures estates, life and liberty to every Dutch inhabitant who shall readily submit to his Government, but those who shall oppose his Majesty's gracious intention must expect all the miseries of a war which they bring on themselves." [1] Stuyvesant offered very little resistance, and Nicolls soon found himself in possession of New Amsterdam. The Dutch West India Company failed to see that they had been largely to blame for leaving their colony inadequately defended, and preferred to pour out the vials of their wrath upon the unfortunate Stuyvesant, who, according to the Company, "first following the example of heedless interested parties, gave himself no other concern than about the prosperity of his

[1] *Calendar of State Papers*, Colonial, 1661-1668, p. 227.

bouweries, and, when the pinch came, allowed himself to be rode over by Clergymen, women and cowards, in order to surrender to the English what he could defend with reputation, for the sake of thus saving their private properties." [1]

The conquest of the main city did not leave Colonel Nicolls idle. The rest of the province had to be subdued, and by his commands the Assistant Commissioner, Cartwright, went forward, took Fort Orange, better known as Albany, and above all laid the foundations of that friendship between the English and the Iroquois which was to prove of such importance in future years. Sir Robert Carr was also sent to take the settlements along the Delaware; but his violence and rapacity in this work contrasted very strongly with the calm and firm rule of Nicolls, and Carr earned for himself unenviable notoriety for his severity, which, it has been said, was "the one exception to the humanity and moderation shown by the English." [2] There were other difficulties which presented themselves to the Governor of New York, not the least being the foundation of New Jersey. James, Duke of York, immediately after the capture of the Dutch settlements, granted all the territory from the Hudson to the Delaware to Sir George Carteret and Lord Berkeley. The district was named New Jersey, and Philip Carteret was sent out by his kinsman to supervise his interests. Nicolls strongly disapproved of this measure; he was a man with a keen political insight, and he saw in this mangling of the province the seed of much commercial and political dispute.

[1] *Documents relative to the Colonial History of the State of New York* (1858).

[2] Doyle, *Cambridge Modern History* (1905), vii. p. 41.

His warning was, of course, unheeded, but that he was right was amply proved by the later history of New Jersey.   Nicolls had also to undo the ill done in Albany by his second in command, Brodhead, who had shown an extraordinary lack of administrative ability, treating the Dutch colonists as an inferior and conquered people, and making numerous arbitrary arrests upon the most trifling charges.   Fortunately for the safety of the colony, news of Brodhead's action reached Nicolls and the despotic deputy was suspended.

The government of New York was no sinecure. It was probably the most cosmopolitan town in North America, and though perhaps it is an exaggeration, it has been asserted that eighteen languages could be heard in the streets of the late Dutch capital.   Before its capture it had become more Anglicised, as Stuyvesant had not feared but favoured the English. The first thing done by Nicolls was to put the town in a state of defence so as to resist any attempt on the part of the Dutch to regain possession, which was essayed by De Ruyter in 1665, but without success. A far more oppressive burden to a man who really had his heart in his work was the difficulty of obtaining supplies for the soldiers.   The English Governor wrote a most pathetic appeal to the Duke of York, telling him how he was paying what he could out of his own pocket, but that the people were starving.   He describes how the inhabitants of Long Island were in terrible poverty, and how New York was in "a mean condition . . . not one soldier has lain in a pair of sheets or on any bed but canvas and straw" since the capture of the town.   He said very pluckily that he did not mind the ruin of his own fortune, but that he could not bear the loss of his reputation; and then, probably to gain his way, he concluded with a delightful sentence of praise that ought to have won the Duke's heart, and which Nicolls no doubt intended that it should. The colony, he writes, exhibited general joy and thanksgiving for the signal victory of the Duke over the Dutch off Lowestoft in June, and for the preservation of His Royal Highness's person, "the very news whereof has revived their spirits and is antidote both against hunger and cold."[1]

Meantime representatives from the English-speaking towns met in February 1665 on Long Island; here, acting in accordance with the wishes of the Governor, a scheme of administration was drawn up; a code of laws was promulgated, and no attempt was made to interfere with the Dutch language. Every town was granted powers of assessment, and the right of choosing a church was given to the freemen who were to declare its denomination. In the cases of the two main Dutch towns of New York and Albany, Nicolls was careful not to arouse ill-feeling, and he allowed them to keep their own mayors. When the first governor retired in 1668, a tribute to his excellent work was paid him by his fellow commissioner Maverick; "he has done his Majesty very considerable service in these parts," he says, "having kept persons of different judgments and divers nations in peace, when a great part of the world was in wars: and as to the Indians, they were never brought into such a peaceable posture and fair correspondence as by his means they now are:"[2]

---

[1] *Calendar of State Papers*, Colonial, 1661-1668, p. 337.
[2] *Ibid.*, p. 606.

Richard Nicolls was succeeded by Francis Lovelace, who had already acted for three years as deputy governor of Long Island. He had before him as governor of New York a far harder task. He followed a man of wonderful power, and it was now his duty to carry on Nicolls' policy and bring the preponderant Dutch population surely but quietly under the but recently established British authority. To accomplish this he adopted a paternal rule ; he granted toleration to all religions ; he attempted to gain the goodwill of the Indians by purchasing their lands and refraining from any action which might be regarded as aggressive. At the same time he helped the colony very considerably by opening up intercourse between New York and Massachusetts, and by the establishment of a regular post between the two capitals. On the other hand, however, Lovelace was not really suited to his post. He was a courtier of the conventional type, and regarded his stay in New York as a form of exile. He speaks of being in " Egyptian darkness," and asks in one of his letters what is stirring on the stage in " Brittang." In writing to Sir Joseph Williamson he tries to arouse his sympathy and says, " we had as well crossed Lethal as the Athlantiq Ocean." The news from home came to him far too seldom, for the conveyance of letters was as slow " as the production of *ellephats*, once almost in two years." [1]

Lovelace's rule soon became unpopular for he was determined to carry out his plan of paternal despotism and resisted very firmly every attempt to create popular representation, which was continually demanded. He angered the settlers by what they

[1] *Calendar of State Papers*, Colonial, 1669-1674, p. III.

regarded a severe tax for defensive purposes, and he showed his contempt for the freeholders of Long Island by ordering their protest against his actions to be burnt.   It was unfortunate that this man should have so alienated both Dutch and English alike, for his period of government coincided with a most critical epoch in the world's history.   In 1670 Charles had allied with Louis XIV. against the Dutch, and one of the first acts of retaliation on the part of the authorities in Holland was to retake their colony of the New Netherlands.   In July 1673 the Dutch Admiral Cornelius Eversen appeared off Fort James when Francis Lovelace was away at New Haven.   The settlers, instead of resisting the Dutch, remembered their hatred of the Governor, and Captain Manning, second in command, having fired one gun, surrendered, an action which was called at the time "a shame and derision to their English nation as hath not been heard of."[1]   Lovelace on his return found the Dutch flag flying over the settlement, and, having no supporters, fled to Long Island, where the English towns had refused to give way, not because of goodwill towards the Governor, but because of patriotism. Here Lovelace met with a scanty welcome and within a few days was arrested, ostensibly on account of a debt owing to the Duke of York, and was sent back to England on the 30th July 1673, where he died soon after.

Weary of a war which was solely for the advantage of the French, Charles II. came to terms with the Dutch at the Treaty of Westminster, 1674.   The New Netherlands once more became New York, but the English ministers made a great error in also restoring

[1] *Calendar of State Papers*, Colonial, 1669-1674, p. 525.

to Carteret and Berkeley their rights in New Jersey. The advice of Nicolls was again neglected, and instead of making New York a compact province, the chance of unity was lost by severing from its jurisdiction the territory of New Jersey. Sir Edmund Andros, who was now appointed governor, did his best to neutralise the effect of this by contending that New Jersey was still tributary to New York, asserting his rights with considerable vigour. But the partners in New Jersey were too great favourites at court to suffer any loss, and before the question was settled Andros was recalled in 1680. His rule was particularly wise and moderate, and during his governorship New York experienced a healthy expansion. One thing, however, he would never grant, though the settlers were always clamouring for it, and that was a clearly defined constitution with political rights and privileges similar to those in the New England colonies.

The exceptionally able Thomas Dongan succeeded Andros, but did not arrive until 1683. He was forced to contend, as will be shown later, with French aggression in the valley of the Hudson ; his method being a firm alliance with the Five Nations or Iroquois. They were a wild and dangerous people, and as such have been described by one who knew them well. " They likewise paint their Faces, red, blue, &c., and then they look like the Devil himself . . . they treat their Enemies with great Cruelty in Time of War, for they first bite off the Nails of the Fingers of their Captives, and cut off some Joints, and sometimes the whole of the Fingers ; after that the Captives are obliged to sing and dance before them . . . and finally they roast them before a slow Fire for some Days, and eat them." It is interesting to note that the writer records what must have been a great relief to his readers in the colonies, that " they are very friendly to us." [1]   This amicable relationship between the English and the Five Nations was largely due to Dongan's good sense and administrative genius.   He persuaded them to become so much subjects of Great Britain as to set up the arms of James II. upon their wigwams.   The English king, when he heard of his governor's action, informed Louis XIV. that, as the Iroquois were now true British subjects, he expected them to be treated as such.   Dongan's work did not stop here.   He was well aware that the Iroquois' friendship was an uncertain prop on which to depend, and therefore palisaded the towns of Albany and Schenectady, thus beginning the famous system of frontier forts.   By his actions he gained the goodwill of the New Yorkers, to whom, on behalf of the Proprietors, he granted a charter of incorporation in 1685.   But this acceptance of the views of the people was only very temporary, as it was reversed in the next year, while at the same time all rights of legislation were vested in a Council appointed by the Crown.

As has already been shown, James II. amalgamated the colonies in 1685 under Sir Edmund Andros and New York became part of New England.   The Governor was kept far too busy in Massachusetts to pay any attention to New York, which was placed under a deputy-governor, Colonel Francis Nicholson, with three Dutch councillors.   Nicholson was a clear-headed, observant man, who had had colonial experience, and would have been a success except for the fact that he lacked moral force.   His position soon became

[1] Hazard, *Historical Collections* (1792).

a very awkward one, for in 1689 he heard that William III. was all-powerful in England, while he held his commission from Andros, the Stuart governor, who was in captivity at Boston. At the same time France had declared war and the Canadians might invade the colony at any moment. Unfortunately for Nicholson, although he summoned the authorities, he quarrelled with his subordinate Cuyler, and things were at a deadlock. At this point the people, seething under the restraints and burdens which had been placed upon them during the reign of James II., rose in open revolt, led by a German brewer, Jacob Leisler. Nicholson was immediately deposed; a convention met, and ten out of the eighteen representatives invested Leisler with dictatorial authority. He was a man of some cunning, and under the pretence of possessing a commission, by intercepting letters and by maltreating their writers, he succeeded in keeping himself in office for very nearly three years. His period of government was distinguished by the first Colonial Congress at Albany, to which he summoned representatives from all the colonies to discuss definite and united action against the French. Leisler himself proposed a joint invasion of Canada, and it is probable that it was only his own arrogance that prevented it. His followers soon came to be as much hated as their leader, and one indignant citizen wrote in January 1690, " never was such a pack of ignorant, scandalous, malicious, false, imprudent, impertinent rascals herded together, out of hell." [1] Careful though Leisler had been to search letters and prevent the news of his usurpation reaching England, he was unsuccessful. In 1690 the English Government

[1] *Calendar of State Papers*, Colonial, 1689-1692, p. 209.

dispatched Colonel Slaughter to take Leisler's place. The usurper was first met by a force under Major Ralph Ingoldsby, second in command to the new Governor; a slight resistance was offered, and Leisler "fired a vast number of great and small shot in the City, whereby several of his Majesty's subjects were killed and wounded as they passed in the streets upon their Lawful Occasions."[1] But Leisler had lost his former following and he was captured and hanged, together with his chief supporter Jacob Millborne.

As James II. had left New York without a constitution, a representative assembly was called in May 1691, and a declaratory act was passed which annulled Leisler's proceedings. It required that all elections in the future should be annual, that the franchise should belong to the 40s. freeholders only, and that the colony itself should be apportioned into constituencies. At the same time it laid down liberty of conscience except for Papists, allowing a declaration instead of an oath to please the Quakers. But above all it declared that no tax was to be imposed unless it was voted by the colony. The act seemed satisfactory enough, except the important reservation with regard to taxation; a reservation which was sufficient to cause the Crown to veto the whole document, and New York was again without a true and defined constitution. Such a state of affairs was particularly bad when the colony in 1692 passed under the rule of the notoriously corrupt Benjamin Fletcher. There are, however, two things to be said for this man, whose work has been spoken of as full of deceit, fraud, and subterfuge. In the first place it has

[1] *A Letter from a Gentleman of the City of New York* (1698).

been proved that in military matters he showed considerable skill and activity; while in the second he undoubtedly realised before many men of his day the danger of disunion. In May 1696 he wrote, "The Indians, though monsters, want not sense, but plainly see we are not united, and it is apparent that the stronger these colonies grow in parts, the weaker we are on the whole, every little government setting up for despotic power and allowing no appeal to the Crown, but valuing themselves on their own strength and on a little juggling in defeating all commands and injunctions of the King."[1]   On the other hand it must be allowed that Fletcher's methods were particularly scandalous, for not only did he practically license smuggling and piracy by levying blackmail upon those who carried on these lucrative trades, but he made personal friends of them, as for example Captain Tew, "a most notorious pirate," with whom, to the scandal of the inhabitants, he occasionally dined.

As has been shown in another chapter, the Earl of Bellomont was made governor in 1698 to prevent these nefarious undertakings, and as ruler of New York, New Jersey, New Hampshire, and Massachusetts he did such good work that he was universally and sincerely regretted when he died in 1701. He was succeeded by Lord Cornbury, who was a profligate in character and overbearing in manner. His rule was one of petty spite and conflict, and having won the especial hatred of the dissenters and generally alienated popular support, his recall in 1708 was as much a cause of rejoicing as Bellomont's death had been of lamentation.

[1] *Calendar of State Papers*, Colonial, 1696-1697, p. 5.

The first sixty years of the eighteenth century were to the inhabitants of New York years of anxiety and peril, for there was the ever present danger of the French to the north and west. The story of these years will be told elsewhere, and here only a rapid sketch can be given of the domestic history of the colony. Four governors or deputy-governors attract particular attention during this period. The first was Governor Burnet,[1] son of the celebrated Bishop, who made himself conspicuous in 1724 by writing a pamphlet in defence of paper money. The governorship of William Cosby was not without a constitutional interest, ten years later, in the prosecution of John Peter Zengler, publisher of the *New York Weekly Journal;* for criticising the government. He was described as a "seditious Person, and a frequent Printer and Publisher of false News and seditious Libels."[2] The same Governor had also a hard struggle with his people, which caused him to write to the home Government for more power and patronage, for "ye example and spirit of the Boston people begins to spread amongst these Colonys In a most prodigious maner, I have had more trouble to manige these people then I could have imagined, however for this time I have done pritty well with them; I wish I may come off as well with them of ye Jarsys."[3]

It is evident that as late as 1740 the position of governor was one of lucrative importance; in that year George Clarke, junior, offered the Duke of

[1] He was also governor of Massachusetts, and died in 1729.

[2] *A Brief Narrative of the Case and Tryal of John Peter Zengler*, etc. (1738).

[3] *Document relative to the Colonial History of the State of New York* (1855).

North, and New Jersey was all the better for a
strong infusion of the vigorous Scottish race.   The
action, too, had the effect of bringing East and West
New Jersey into closer contact, and so paved the way
for union.   In 1692 another step was taken in this
direction, for the Proprietors of both colonies appointed
Andrew Hamilton as joint-governor.   There were,
however, many difficulties to be overcome before
union was possible.   In the first place there were
unending disputes with New York about the levying
of duties ; while secondly, the Proprietors' rights had
now become so complicated by frequent sale and
transfer that matters were in dire confusion ; besides
these very rights appeared to the settlers themselves
as injurious to the welfare of the colony.   They
looked for political privileges for themselves, which
would, according to the Proprietors, clash with their
interests.   To grant to the settlers rights which were
on the surface merely political, appeared, and indeed
would be, the abnegation of all proprietary territorial
claims.   The man who might have done so much for
the union of the New Jerseys had unfortunately transferred his affections elsewhere.   Penn, filled with
schemes of pure philanthropy, had left his first
settlement to look after itself and had brought
all his energies to bear upon his new venture in
Pennsylvania.

Even without Penn's assistance the union of the
two Jerseys was bound to come.   In 1701 it was
pointed out by the Colonial Office of that day, that
" by several letters, memorials, and other papers, as
well from the inhabitants as Proprietors of both these
provinces, that they are at present in confusion and
anarchy ; and that it is much to be apprehended lest

by the heats of the parties that are amongst them, they should fall into such violences as may endanger the lives of many persons and destroy the colony."[1]   It seemed obvious to those in London that some form of union was necessary to save the colony from this fate, and so New Jersey from the River Hudson to the River Delaware became a united province when the Proprietors surrendered all their political and territorial rights in 1702.   For a short time New Jersey with New York suffered under the scandalous administration of the brainless and profligate Lord Cornbury, but his evil work was to a certain extent remedied by Governor Robert Hunter, who proved himself an able colonial administrator.

The tract of land to which Penn had transferred his philanthropic schemes lay to the south of the river Delaware.   It had been taken from the Swedes and at one time had been granted to Maryland, but up to the year 1681 it had remained unoccupied.   The Quaker Penn, a man of high social position, friend and favourite of James II., readily accepted this piece of territory in liquidation of a debt of £16,000 owed to him by the Crown.   The agreement now drawn up between Penn and the Duke of York was remarkable for its utter indifference to all constitutional forms. Penn was appointed Proprietor, but his powers were to a certain extent limited ; on all legislative matters the Crown reserved the right of veto, and in all financial affairs the newly formed colony was to be regarded as an integral portion of the realm ; while, as a further hold over revenue, an accredited agent of the colony was to reside in England and was to explain any infraction of the revenue laws.

[1] Compare the *N.J. Archives*, ii., p. 420.

Pennsylvania, as first conceived by the Proprietor, was not a colony for one sect only. He offered no particular inducements to Quakers rather than to others. The early emigrants were a veritable olla podrida, and consisted of English Quakers, Scottish and Irish Presbyterians, German Mennonites, and French Huguenots. It was not long, however, before the Quaker element distinctly preponderated, with two obvious results. In the first place one of the strongest tenets of Quakerism was a horror of war and bloodshed, which belief was steadily upheld by the Pennsylvanians and proved in later years most baneful to the colony when the French began their aggressions. The second result was just as good as the first had been bad. The Quakers taught and believed the equality of all men before God ; to them there was no distinction between settler and savage, and unlike some of the colonists in the Puritan group, offered the best of treatment to the Red Indians.

In the autumn of 1681, William Penn dispatched four commissioners to found the colony that was in later years to become so famous. William Crispen, Nathaniel Allen, John Bezar and William Heage were chosen by the Proprietor to select a site on the Delaware ; Crispen, Penn's kinsman, died on the voyage, but the other three faithfully carried out their orders and selected a spot where the river " is most navigable, high dry and healthy ; that is where most ships can ride, of deepest draught of water, if possible to load or unload at the bank or key (*sic*) side without boating or lightering of it." [1] Thomas Howe had been appointed surveyor-general and at once proceeded to lay out the city of Philadelphia upon a modification

[1] Quoted in the *Enc. Britannica.*

of the plans of Penn and covering a surface area of about 1200 to 1300 acres. William Penn stands alone as the founder of a great city of which he was justly proud, and in 1683 he was able to write, " Philadelphia : the expectation of those who are concerned in this province is at last laid out, to the great content of those here who are anyways interested therein. The situation is a neck of land and lieth between two navigable rivers, Delaware and Sculkill, whereby it hath two fronts upon the water, each a mile, and two from river to river." [1]

Penn was quick to foresee a prosperous future for his colony, but he nearly ruined it at the outset by drawing up a well-intentioned but somewhat cumbersome constitution. There were to be two elective chambers : the Upper or council, consisting of 72 members, and the Lower, which was at first to contain 200, and later 500 members. This constitution, however, was impossible to manage ; the Lower assembly was obviously far too large and proved superfluous ; while the Upper was found to be too bulky for a Cabinet or executive government ; for these reasons a few months after its conception it was radically altered. The pruning-knife was called into use and the 72 of the Upper chamber were cut down to 18 ; at the same time the absurd number of 200 was reduced to 26, and the right of initiating legislation was taken from the representatives. But Penn was not yet satisfied and undertook still further alterations in 1686, when he appointed five Commissioners of State, three of whom were to be a quorum, and to whom the right of veto in all legislative affairs was granted. This scheme was almost as bad as his first

[1] Janney, *Life of William Penn* (1852).

constitution, for it gave excessive powers to three or four men; fortunately for the colony it was not perpetuated.

Early in its history troubles came upon Pennsylvania, which had been founded " with the pious wish and desire that its inhabitants might dwell together in brotherly love and unity." [1] The flight of James II. was the first serious blow to Penn's colonial prosperity; it may be that he was one of the few men who sincerely and deeply regretted the fall of the last male Stuart ruler of England, for in James' misfortune Penn also suffered for a time, and his plans as a colony promoter received a severe check. At the same time Pennsylvania was torn by internal quarrels concerning what were called the " Territories " or Delaware. This district, on the south bank of the Delaware River, had been transferred from the administration of New York and placed under that of Pennsylvania. The dispute that arose had for its cause the appointment of magistrates, and it was only settled by a compromise in which Delaware was for the future to have its own executive, but there was only to be one elective chamber for the whole province. Still worse days came to Pennsylvania when the colony was included in the commission to the pirate-loving Benjamin Fletcher. As in New York, so in the Quaker settlement he proved himself arbitrary in conduct, brutal and unwise in action, immoral and corrupt in his private life. The only comfort to the Pennsylvanian settlers during his rule was that they won their right to initiate legislation.

A promise of the renewal of the good days of the past appeared when Penn succeeded in 1694 in re-

---

[1] Pastorius, *Geographical Description of Pennsylvania* (1850).

gaining his proprietary rights, now somewhat shorn of their former privileges. The Proprietor immediately set about the restoration of his colony's prosperity, but excellent as his work was, Pennsylvania was still more fortunate in having amongst its members Gabriel Thomas, one of the brightest colonial authors of that period. He has not only left some writings of particular merit, but his name has been handed down to posterity as one who laboured hard for seventeen years to build up, firmly and strongly, the Quaker settlements in the West. Such work was necessarily slow, and Penn, when he again visited his colony, must have been much grieved with its moral condition if Lewis Morris, Governor of New Jersey, wrote the truth. "Pennsylvania is settled by People of all Languages and Religions in Europe, but the people called Quakers are the most numerous of anyone persuasion . . . the Church of England gains ground in that Country, and most of the Quakers that came off with Mr Keith are come over to it : the Youth of that country are like those in the neighbouring Provinces very Debaucht and ignorant."[1]

A long series of disputes with the other colonies began in 1701, which intensified the danger already only too obvious, caused by the disunion of the American states and left them the more open to French attack. In addition to their antipathy to war, the Pennsylvanians now pleaded poverty as an excuse for refusing to assist in contributing funds towards the restoration of the fortifications of New York. Penn's common sense forced him to advocate the contribution, but all his eloquence was wasted upon his settlers, and he pleaded and remonstrated in

[1] New Jersey Historical Society, *Proceedings* (1849-1850).

vain. A fresh dispute followed, again arising from the government of Delaware. Since the last quarrel the Assembly had met alternately at Newcastle and Philadelphia. The people of Pennsylvania, as members of the more important state, demanded that in the future any legislation passed at Newcastle should be ratified and confirmed at Philadelphia. This was naturally intolerable to the weaker side, and the outcome of the dispute was the granting of a new charter and the complete separation of Delaware in 1703.

The last official act of William Penn was the incorporation of his beloved city of Philadelphia, which had steadily increased in size and population. A contemporary in 1710, possibly Daniel Defoe, has left on record a description of the town which gives some idea of its character and importance. Philadelphia "is a noble, large and populous city, standing on as much ground as our English City of Bristol. . . . It is built square in Form of a Chess-Board with each Front facing one of the Rivers. There are several Streets near two Mile long, as wide as Holborn, and better built, after the English Manner. The chief are Broad Street, King-street, High-street, tho' there are several other handsome Streets that take their Names from the Productions of the Country : as Mulberry, Walnut, Beech, Sassafras, Cedar, Vine, Ash and Chestnut Streets. . . . The Number of the Inhabitants is generally suppos'd to be upwards of 15,000 besides Slaves. . . . And if I were oblig'd to live out of my native Country, I should not be long puzzled in finding a Place of Retirement, which should be Philadelphia. There the oppress'd in Fortune or Principles may find a happy Asylum, and drop quietly to their Graves without Fear or Want."[1] Such was the happy city within thirty years of its foundation, and as a political centre it remained supreme until after the American War of Independence.

Penn retired from the colony in 1701, but continued to take the keenest interest in all that went on. At one time he remonstrated with the assembly for attacking his secretary and staunch supporter, James Logan, who acted as the Proprietor's agent during his long years of absence. As long as Penn lived he was able to exercise some control, but when he died in 1718 he left to his heirs a proprietary claim over a colony torn in pieces by disputes and factions. The brothers John and Thomas Penn were never popular, and up to the resignation of their claims in 1759 there were continual quarrels, sometimes over the Governor's salary, and sometimes because the Proprietors, who possessed three-fourths of the province, refused to allow the taxation of their lands for military operations against the French.

It is a noticeable fact that the two last colonies of the famous Thirteen were founded on philanthropic bases. The excellent William Penn established Pennsylvania as a home of toleration and peace ; and the last of the original states, Georgia, was founded upon motives that were highly creditable to their originator. The colony of Georgia owed its existence to James Oglethorpe, who, after serving a short time in the army, became a Member of Parliament and was placed upon a Parliamentary Committee to inquire into the state of the prisons, at that time conducted on barbarous lines. What he then learnt led Oglethorpe to propose the formation of a colony where

[1] *The Voyages and Adventures of Captain Robert Boyle*, etc. (1726).

men might honestly work and better their position instead of pining away in the horrible debtors' gaols. In addition to this, as he said, " Christianity will be extended by the execution of this design ; since the good discipline established by the Society will reform the manners of these miserable objects." [1]   There is, too, in his account of the advantages of the colony, a hint as to the possible pecuniary gain of the individual and of the nation, for " when hereafter it shall be well-peopled and rightly cultivated, England may be supplied from thence with raw Silk, Wine, Oil, Dyes, Drugs, and many other materials for manufactures, which she is obliged to purchase from Southern countries." [2]   Tempted by these proposals, the Government readily fell in with his scheme and granted to Oglethorpe and his associates, including the famous Thomas Coram, a tract of land to the south of the Savannah River and north of the Spanish settlements in Florida, and here the debtors' colony was to serve as a barrier and rampart against Spanish aggression. The Corporation was called " The Trustees for the colonisation of Georgia," and was given full powers of administration for twenty-six years, at the expiration of which all privileges were to pass to the Crown.

In the autumn of 1732, James Oglethorpe embarked with 114 settlers ; they were unsatisfactory colonists, for the men who had so hopelessly failed in England had not that grit and sturdy endurance necessary for founders of new homes in the West. The colony, however, started well, for Oglethorpe immediately won the goodwill of the natives, and made a wise selection of a site for the first settlement about twenty miles

[1] Force, *Tracts* (1836).   [2] *Ibid.*

from the mouth of the Savannah River. The town itself was guarded on the water side by high banks, while impenetrable swamps on the land side served as sufficient barrier to any warlike incursions that might be attempted. Besides these advantages, Oglethorpe had also made friendly overtures to the neighbouring colonies, and in 1733 was able to say with satisfaction that " if the colony is attacked it may be relieved by sea from Port Royal, or the Bahamas ; and the militia of South Carolina is ready to support it, by land." [1] Oglethorpe's satisfaction must have been very short-lived. From the very first the colonists grumbled, quarrelled, and disputed, and their resident minister, the Reverend Samuel Quincy, gives a horrible but exaggerated account of the colony in 1735. " Affairs here are but in an ill-condition, through the discouragements attending the settlement. . . . The magistrate, to whom the government of the colony was left, proves a most insolent and tyrannical fellow. Several just complaints have been sent home against him, which do not meet with a proper regard, and this has made people very uneasie. . . . In short, Georgia, which was seemingly intended to be the asylum of the distressed, unless things are greatly altered, is likely to be itself a mere scene of distress. . . . Notwithstanding the place has been settled nigh three years, I believe, I may venture to say there is not one family which can subsist without further assistance." [2] Affairs though gloomy were scarcely as black as Quincy depicted them, for in the next few years there was every sign of progress. Already in 1734 there had been a large increase of population by the

[1] Force, *Tracts* (1836).
[2] Massachusetts Historical Society, *Collections* (1814).

immigration of Salzburg Germans under their pastor Martin Bolzius, who had fled from the persecution of their Prince Bishop. Two years later the colony had grown sufficiently to found a second settlement, Frederica, seventy miles south of the Savannah, at the mouth of the Alatamaha River ; and a party of Highlanders about the same time founded New Inverness. Trade also began to increase and a definite commercial station was established at Augusta.

In the same year as the foundation of Frederica, John Wesley, accompanied by his brother Charles, came out as chaplain to the Georgian flock. He was in residence for a year and nine months, during which period he seems to have quarrelled with many of the inhabitants and particularly with the Moravians, and proved himself both indiscreet and ill-tempered. He himself records in his *Journal* that he was told by one man, " I will never hear you any more. And all the people are of my mind. For we won't hear ourselves abused. Besides, they say, they are Protestants. But as for you, they can't tell what Religion you are of. They never heard of such a religion before. They do not know what to make of it. And then, your private behaviour—all the quarrels that have been here since you came, have been long of you. Indeed there is neither man nor woman in the Town, who minds a word you say. And so you may preach long enough ; but nobody will come to hear you." [1] Wesley seems to have allowed his own personal feelings to enter into his religious life. He desired to marry a young woman of his congregation, Sophia Hankey by name, but she preferred to marry a Mr

[1] Wesley, *Journal*, June 22, 1736.

Williamson. Thereupon, apparently without any other reason than his own personal feelings, Wesley excluded Mrs Williamson from communion. Her husband very naturally regarded this as a slur upon his wife's character and brought an action against Wesley, who was forbidden to leave the colony while the question was pending. He records in his *Journal* for December 2nd what then took place. " In the Afternoon the Magistrates publish'd an Order requiring all the Officers and Centinels, to prevent my going out of the Province ; and forbidding any person to assist me so to do. Being now only a Prisoner at large, in a Place, where I knew by experience every Day would give fresh opportunity, to procure Evidence of words I never said, and actions I never did ; I saw clearly the Hour was come for leaving the Place : And as soon as Evening Prayers were over, about Eight o'clock, the tide then serving, I shook off the dust of my Feet, and left Georgia, after having preach'd the Gospel there (not as I ought but as I was able) one Year and nearly Nine Months." [1]   In regarding Wesley's action at this time, it is to be remembered that he was a self-confident, impulsive young enthusiast, lacking knowledge of human nature, and also that he had not passed through those years of struggle and earnest work which in later times made him a man of tact and forbearance.

Meantime a serious danger threatened the colony. In 1736, the Spaniards, who had long viewed Georgia with suspicion, made an armed reconnaissance, but nothing could be done, for there was at that time no war between the two countries in Europe. It was not until 1739 that Walpole was forced by popular

[1] Wesley, *Journal*, December 2, 1737.

demand to declare war against Spain, an act which he
regarded with disgust as contrary to all his principles
and desires. Georgia was in a particularly exposed
position with regard to Spanish aggression, and
Oglethorpe decided to take the offensive as a defensive measure and carry the war into the enemy's
country. Reading the signs of the times and knowing
what was hatching in Europe, the English Governor
collected a force of about 600 volunteers and
boldly marched for Florida in October 1738. He
had been partly led to this action by the fact that
news had been brought that the Spanish troops had
been increased in St Augustine, and that the civil
inhabitants had been turned out of their houses to
give quarters to the royal forces. Oglethorpe's move
was an unsatisfactory one, not through want of bravery
on his part, but rather because he was a poor judge of
men and his soldiers were wanting in the spirit of
loyalty; some had even concerted a plot with the
Spanish, while others had actually deserted to the
enemy. Nothing daunted, Oglethorpe spent the
summer of 1739 securing the alliance of most of the
neighbouring Indian tribes, and when war was formally
declared against Spain the Georgian Governor was in
a better position for whatever fate might have in
store.

The home authorities ordered Oglethorpe to attack
St Augustine, but before he could do so the Spaniards
struck the first blow. Some fifty miles south of the
town of Frederica, the Governor had thought it advis-
able to erect a military station on Amelia Island.
This was the first natural object of Spanish attack, but
their success was limited to the murder of two invalids.
Oglethorpe, on the other hand, was more fortunate in

L

capturing a Spanish outpost, which tempted him to risk an attack on St Augustine itself. He set out in March 1740, with a land force of about 2000 men, composed of Georgian militia and Indian allies; being supported at sea by four King's ships and a small schooner from South Carolina. This latter was practically the only help from the members of the richer colony, the generosity of which was of a very limited character; they ought really to have assisted Oglethorpe as well as they were able, for their danger from the Spaniards was almost as extreme as that of Georgia. Ill-supported as he was, the Governor captured three small fortresses, but soon found that the seizure of the capital of Florida was beyond his slender resources. The few Carolina troops deserted; his own men were struck down by fever; and his Indian allies left him in disgust because he tried to restrain their natural ferocity. In June, having realised that his attempt was hopeless, he retreated. His work, however, was not entirely unsuccessful, for although he had failed to do what he had intended, he succeeded in staving off from Georgia any serious Spanish attack for the next two years.

The year 1742 marks the crisis of Oglethorpe's career, for it was then that he won for himself a reputation for daring and strategy. The Spaniards attacked the colony and, knowing of their approach by means of his Indian allies, Oglethorpe concentrated all his forces upon the town of Frederica. The Spanish vanguard made an impetuous onslaught against which the Governor led with considerable daring his own ill-organised men. He showed that spirit of courage and prowess that fascinated even his

wretched followers, who gave him willingly what
support they could.   He himself captured single-
handed two of the Spaniards.   But his strategy was
yet to be displayed.   As the fight continued, he sent
through the wood a flank force which fell upon the
Spaniards so suddenly and unexpectedly that they
were routed with heavy loss, and the panic was
sustained by an expedient of Oglethorpe's invention.
By means of a deserter he succeeded in hoodwinking
the enemy, declaring that he was ready for a second
assault, which would be welcomed with the same
hearty spirit that had been accorded to the first ; at
the same time he informed them, in mere bravado,
that he was expecting an English fleet.   As a matter
of fact the desire for a second attack and the arrival
of English vessels were mere figments of Oglethorpe's
imagination.   But as the gods fight on the side of the
brave, so Oglethorpe was rewarded by the almost
miraculous appearance of a few men-of-war.   From
that moment Georgia may be said to have earned her
safety.   She owed her existence to Oglethorpe, and to
him and his cunning she owed her salvation.   It may
be truly said that at last the colony had thoroughly
justified its existence and had fulfilled one of the main
functions for which it had been created.   The afore-
time debtors of England had not shown particular
courage, but their leader had fulfilled the promise of
ten years before, and Georgia had stood firm and
strong as a bulwark defending its more prosperous
neighbours who lay upon the northern frontier.
Those neighbours had much for which to thank the
weakly colony, to whom in time of stress they had
given little or no assistance.   It was only one more
example of the lack of unity, and one more instance of

that failure to secure really effective co-operation
which, had it existed, would have made so great a
difference to the advance of the colonies. Georgia's
position was, however, all the more exalted, for under
Oglethorpe she had stood alone and had not been
found wanting.

The colony was now safe from invasion, but there
were many internal difficulties that had to be confronted. The debtors of England were not like the
hardy and cheerful Salzburgers who managed to flourish
and enjoy life. The climate itself was one of the
most serious drawbacks to white labour, and an
influential party saw that the colony could hardly
compete against the other southern states where
slave labour was employed. This party was supported in its views by George Whitefield, who had
come to Georgia in 1738 and who strongly advocated
negro slavery. When it is remembered that one of
the most permanent triumphs of the Evangelical party
was the abolition of slavery, it is curious that one of
the earliest and greatest of its leaders should have
defended and encouraged the slave owners. But his
advocacy had no effect upon the Trustees, who were
firm in their determination to prevent negro slave
traffic. The settlers sent a strong protest to England
in 1739, stating that "Timber is the only thing we
have here . . . yet we cannot manufacture it for a
Foreign Market but at double the Expense of other
Colonies ; as for Instance, the River of May, which
is but twenty miles from us, with the Allowance of
negroes, load Vessels with that Commodity at one
Half of the Price that we can do. . . . We are very
sensible of the Inconveniences and Mischiefs that have
already, and do daily arise from an unlimited Use of

Negroes ; but we are as sensible, that these may be prevented by a due Limitation."[1] The Trustees replied that the introduction of negroes would be the introduction of a "baneful Commodity, which, it is well known by sad Experience, has brought our Neighbour Colonies to the Brink of Ruin, by driving out their White Inhabitants, who were their Glory and Strength, to make room for Black, who are now become the Terror of their unadvised Masters."[2] Excellent as the answer of the Trustees was, there can be little doubt that for lack of proper executive both the restrictions on liquor and on slavery were systematically evaded and after 1752 were allowed to lapse.

Oglethorpe, promoted to the rank of General, left Georgia in 1743, never to return. The colony cannot be called an entire success ; the very philanthropy upon which it was founded deprived it to a certain extent of those enduring qualities which had made the New England colonies strong and healthy provinces. But though Oglethorpe had not accomplished all that he had wanted to do, a modern writer has paid him a high tribute when he says that he "had attained a far larger measure of success than most men could have won with such material."[3] That the colony was prospering is shown by Edmund Burke in 1759, when he said, "At present Georgia is beginning to emerge, though slowly, out of the difficulties that attended its first establishment : It is still but indifferently peopled, though it is now twenty-six years since its first settlement. Not one of our colonies was of so slow a growth, though none had

---

[1] Force, *Tracts* (1836).   [2] *Ibid.*
[3] Doyle, *Cambridge Modern History* (1905), vol. vii. p. 63.

so much of the attention of the Government, or of the people in general, or raised so great expectations in the beginning. They export some corn and lumber to the West Indies ; they raise some rice, and of late are going with success into indigo. It is not to be doubted but in time, when their internal divisions are a little better composed, the remaining errors in the government corrected, and the people begin to multiply, that they will become a useful province." [1]

Some of the " errors in the government " had come up for discussion as early as 1751, when for the first time a representative assembly was called, but it was only granted deliberative functions. The whole character of the government of Georgia was radically altered when, according to the original agreement, the colony passed into the hands of the Crown. The population now consisted of 2380 whites and 1060 negroes, and these came to be governed under a constitution of normal type consisting of a governor, council, and executive officers nominated by the Crown, and a representative assembly elected by the freeholders.

Such, then, was the history of the last colony to be founded, completing the unlucky number thirteen, and it remained the weakest and least efficient of all. From small beginnings the English colonies came into being along the Eastern seaboard of America. Puritans and cavaliers, profligates and mechanics, all helped to create what might have been except for sad misunderstandings part of the British empire of to-day. Behind the Alleghany slopes another great power was attempting to form a colonial empire. North of the St Lawrence, New France had already

[1] *An Account of the European Settlements in America* (1760).

WILLIAM PITT, FIRST EARL OF CHATHAM

FROM THE PAINTING BY W. HOARE IN THE NATIONAL PORTRAIT GALLERY